Managing High-Stakes Risk

Managing High-Stakes Risk

Toward a New Economics for Survival

Mark Jablonowski

First published 2009 by
PALGRAVE MACMILLAN

Palgrave Macmillan in the UK is an imprint of Macmillan Publishers Limited, registered in England, company number 785998, of Houndmills, Basingstoke, Hampshire RG21 6XS.

Palgrave Macmillan in the US is a division of St Martin's Press LLC, 175 Fifth Avenue, New York, NY 10010.

Palgrave Macmillan is the global academic imprint of the above companies and has companies and representatives throughout the world.

Palgrave® and Macmillan® are registered trademarks in the United States, the United Kingdom, Europe and other countries.

ISBN-13: 978–0–230–23827–5 hardback

This book is printed on paper suitable for recycling and made from fully managed and sustained forest sources. Logging, pulping and manufacturing processes are expected to conform to the environmental regulations of the country of origin.

A catalogue record for this book is available from the British Library.

A catalog record for this book is available from the Library of Congress.

10   9   8   7   6   5   4   3   2   1
18   17   16   15   14   13   12   11   10   09

Printed and bound in Great Britain by
CPI Antony Rowe, Chippenham and Eastbourne

Contents

Preface: Does Our Existence Matter?

Intuitively, survival sounds like a very sound goal. At least we might all agree on the fact that survival is better than extinction. Some may suggest that the continuing human presence on earth provides at least some indication that our existence *does* matter to us. Yet, what about the future? While it may seem like survival is important to us, it is also becoming increasingly evident that, with respect to incurring existential threats, people accept the idea that "there is no choice" far too easily. The paradox that results is that we can achieve utopia, including the ultimate fruits of progress, only under the threat of extinction.

We might also agree that a completely risk-free life is simply not consistent with the way the physical world is. Practically, zero risk is unachievable, by the very laws of nature. Yet, a reasonable goal for a safer world might include achieving and maintaining risk at a natural risk level, assuring some minimum level of comfort. Such natural risk levels are, after all, consistent with a rather remarkable streak of human evolution. Nonetheless, we are by most indications very far from such natural levels today.

What about the technicalities of achieving a safer world? We might also quite reasonably believe that by setting appropriate risk goals, we could adequately plan for the achievement of such goals. Integrating survival planning into a system of social and economic planning seems like a perfect fit. A carefully planned course of action can help preserve survival against the increased complexities of progress. Yet recognizing the value of planning is not enough. We need the impetus to *do it*.

Clearly, achieving a safer world requires understanding the "why's" as well as the "how's" of survival. And that suggests that a deeper look into the philosophy of our existence is in order. Against the backdrop of moral commitments, to ourselves, other humans, and the natural environment that supports us, we can start to discern what actions really make sense when it comes to survival. Once we understand what it is we truly value, or should value, the impediments to achieving these ends become more apparent. These impediments may be practical, in the sense of doing what it takes to plan for more natural risk levels, or they may lie deeper within the human psyche. We therefore need to also understand what factors within *ourselves* may hinder the achievement of what we really value.

In the end, our actions will speak louder than words. The question of whether our existence matters will be answered by what we do. If we notice an inconsistency which we just can't live with, literally or figuratively, we need to take actions for change. We would suggest that these actions are, quite simply, based on coordinated planning for the achievement of natural risk levels. We would further argue that these actions are the *only* ones consistent with a philosophy of life that coordinates our existence with some sort of natural order, or what we ultimately call "fate". On the other hand, we may choose to live with distortions of this philosophy, either foisted on us by others or which may perhaps be an unchangeable part of the human condition. We may even be fooled into considering current happiness as a suitable tradeoff for future existence. Doing so, we must at least recognize that such bargains may ultimately end our existence, or at least eventually make it a very unpleasant one.

In the discussion that follows, we present a realistic approach to the understanding of high-stakes risks, and their treatment. This presentation does not rely on scientific proofs, mathematical constructs, or carefully constructed experiments. In this sense, it is meant to be intuitive, in that it is based on extended experience. Risk is a physical property of the world. How we perceive and respond to such physical properties is what life is all about. This also means that it is up to all of us to have at least some understanding of the issues when it comes to the risks of our existence. In this world of specialization we have a tendency to leave even the most important things to others. We depend on others, either by commercial or social contract, to provide the guidance needed, when needed. With respect to risk, that means that we often feel that "someone else" is looking after us – another individual, a business, or the government. That may or may not be the case. To become too dependent on others for our existence in our current *laissez faire* world is a dangerous gambit. At the very least, it assumes everyone else cares, or can be made to care, about our existence as much as we do. We have to figure out if existence matters for ourselves. Once we do, we cannot simply rely on all others to be of like mind. That said, we can't do it all by ourselves. In this world, some dependence on others is unavoidable. The unifying thread then is what we call here a *sense of purpose*. That means trying to understand where we fit into the wider scope of life. Once we recognize that sense of purpose, or are made to do so, we can then collectively work to achieve it.

This work offers, unapologetically, a possible framework for achieving some degree of concrete utopia. By that we mean an existence where our belonging makes sense, and in the process of this recognition we achieve maximum satisfaction. It is a rational view of what living the best life really means. The idea being that if we understand it all, even if that understanding entails identifying areas where that understanding is imperfect (i.e., knowing what we don't know), it brings with it a sense of peace. We at least achieve enough comfort to face whatever it is that this life has in store for us. In this sense, the idea of fate remains absolutely crucial to our existence. What will be, will be. The link between fate and utopia is being able to face what will be with the comfort that we did everything rationally possible to achieve a respectable life, regardless of how it turns out. Living a life within this natural order becomes its own reward – its own utopia.

Science and morals, and the values they entail, have to come together in any sensible discussion of high-stakes risks. A scientific understanding of the risk we face is worthless without a moral framework, and vice versa. The study of high-stakes risk is not all about deep principles and the way things should be. It is about how they are now, and how we go about setting them on the right track, if need be. The immediate nature of the endeavor, this concentration on what we might call the *viability* of utopia, is what makes this book practical. The content is meant to be digested, argued, distilled, and, ultimately, *used*.

Modern life is defined by social patterns of production, distribution, and consumption of the goods and services that define the "good life": In a word, *economics*. Managing existential risk is therefore inextricably bound to the economics of modern life. It is in the tradition of the study of economic systems that we present a "new" system for assuring survival in a world of risk. In the end, we show that the very human process of economic activity needs to become more natural in its ends and means if it is to proceed in harmony with the wider environment.

1
The Philosophy of *Survival*

This book is about facing threats that we know little about, and yet can have enormous consequences. We face uncertain, random events every day. The critical distinction we make here is between the more mundane, day-to-day risks and those that affect our very survival. The focus on catastrophic, or what we might generally call *high-stakes* risks, brings an existential character to an otherwise technical discussion. We emphasize this existential character because it affects not only the methods of risk management, but also how we view its goals. In this first chapter, we identify issues in the philosophy of existence (our own and that of other sentient beings that we depend on), including the idea of purpose and our ability to *know* that purpose.

In simplest terms, risk management is about reducing worry. The goals of the endeavor are made complex when we try to identify what we are, or should be, most worried about. The complexities of this whole endeavor add a layer of uncertainty beyond mere chance. The implication of imperfect knowledge of our world, and even our place in this world, makes our journey into the unknown all that more perilous. As it turns out, a respect for a more natural approach to the world, guided by properly honed intuitions, may serve as our best guide to navigating through a world in which many aspects are beyond our direct control.

1.1   Ethics and the treatment of existential risk

A key feature of dealing with existential risk is that it requires a deeper philosophy of risk, and, indeed, existence. As risk is itself something humans create, or at least respond to in different ways, it behooves us to establish a moral attitude toward risk – a *survival ethic*. That is, we need to determine the difference between right and wrong behavior, especially with respect to other entities that may be affected. In turn, our moral approach to risk strongly influences the technical aspects of how we deal with risk. Once settled, our morals become the basis of a system of ethics and ethical behavior.

Moral philosophy usually splits along two lines. The first deals with basic intuitions of how we *ought* to respond to this world, with actual outcomes, or consequences, being secondary. This stance is often referred to as *deontological*. Its ethic of survival boils down to simply doing the right thing. On the other hand, *consequentialism* says that all our goals are ultimately focused on observable ends. In the management of risk, consequentialism is often applied on a utilitarian basis. That is, all acts, including those that entail risk, are ultimately judged by the direct satisfaction, or utility, they provide to those sentient beings that can experience such satisfaction. The idea of utility as a measurable quantity of satisfaction also introduces the idea of tradeoffs. In living our lives to the fullest, we often make tradeoffs among goals, or in the use of otherwise scarce resources, in order to get the most satisfaction from our actions.

Utility-based consequentialism is all about optimizing, or getting the most, from our actions.

Utilitarianism therefore amounts to a rational optimization of satisfaction. When dealing with day-to-day, statistical risks the utilitarian approach is easily applied. The outcome of our actions can be readily judged, albeit only "on average" (due to randomness), or over some long run. When dealing with existential risks, some would argue that a deeper meaning of existence is sought. This meaning is often couched in a deontological perspective. Existence has a meaning beyond mere individual experience, so should our approach to it.

Many observers suggest that consequentialism and deontology are distinct, and indeed, incompatible, approaches to decisions about life. Deontology has been defined by some as those moral choices we make that are *not* based simply on consequences. Although the friction between consequentialism and deontology has a long philosophical and practical history, we take the stand here that both consequentialism, or more specifically utilitarianism, and deontology are part of the wider idea of *teleology*, or the study of purpose, or goals. This sense of purpose, in turn, guides our ethical and moral responses to the world, including those that deal with survival. To determine the proper approach to life, we need to understand its *telos*, or purpose. The identification of both utilitarianism and deontology as falling within the scope of teleology means that they both require us to identify, if not the purpose of life in all its glorious detail, at least the idea that such purpose exists. The wider view of value follows from respecting this purpose. On this basis, we argue that deontology, what ought to be done, requires conforming to some outcome. While not directly consequential, it must be at least purposive. We exist for a reason, even though we may not be completely clear of that reason. Therefore, we need to respect the parameters of this existence, however vague the reasons for it may appear to us.

Our approach focuses on the principle that while all action is ultimately based on consequences, the teleology that underlies these consequences is extremely complex. It depends on wider natural, or perhaps, what we might call *cosmic*, laws which we cannot identify the precise meaning of. As such, life is about determining how to best fit into this cosmic whole. The complexity, and the uncertainty it entails, suggests that a great deal of where we end up is up to fate. Fate here is taken to mean the working of this complex world, or cosmos, in which we live. In the words of the Stoic philosopher Chrysippus, who lived in the first century BC, fate may be defined as

> ...a certain natural arrangement of the universe, with things following upon other things and being involved with other things from eternity, such a weaving being inexorable....

A *deontology of survival*, therefore, follows from this view of fate as natural, or cosmic, order. It prescribes absolute rules that are required to live in harmony with these natural laws. It follows then that this harmonious existence is its own ultimate reward. So while a natural view of the world promotes a sort of consequentialism, it is based on a very complex, and imperfectly observable, notion of purpose. The absolutes it entails, in terms of following this natural order, themselves naturally fit within the framework of deontology, or how we *ought* to live our lives.

In its statistical sense, when dealing with the more mundane aspect of the world, the underlying deontology does not make much difference. It is captured wholly in the idea of readily observable outcomes, and the possibility of sensible tradeoffs. We can handle the mechanics of statistical decision using the well-developed theory of probability. Valuation of these tradeoffs is straightforward as well, and it entails the economist's notion of utility, or satisfaction. Decisions are made based on a weighing of costs and benefits, in terms of utility, with an eye toward maximizing satisfaction in the long run. However, long–run arguments about statistical tradeoffs simply do no make sense when dealing with absolutes, like survival. We need to adjust our decisions accordingly. When decisions become existential, especially when they involve not only individuals but economic systems, societies, or even the ecosphere itself, we need to introduce a wider philosophical perspective. It is a perspective that may be most simply captured in Hamlet's famous query, "To be or not to be?" Obviously, we enter a realm outside of pure calculation of costs and benefits. Or, at least, we need to carefully redefine the notion of costs and benefits to deal with the seriousness of the task.

1.2   Moral absolutes, values and the commitment to a natural order

The philosophy of moral absolutes takes perhaps its most refined form in the eighteenth-century moral philosopher Immanuel Kant's *categorical imperative*. Kant suggested that absolute moral principles are those we would treat as universal laws. The key then to moral maxims is their *universalizability*. While Kant's own moral philosophy placed ends over means, it is hard not to conceive of moral quality as having at least some connection to the real world, or to real results in that world. We would argue that deontology without some *telos*, some sense of purpose, is barren. In this way, we can avoid a deontology that simply becomes a foundation for a moralistic position that values rhetoric over substantial change. Absolutes, however, do not automatically translate into obligations. So while we maintain the idea of moral absolutes as applied to the avoidance of existential risks, we do so based on maintaining a realizable natural order. This natural order follows from a flow of the universe which we disturb at our peril. Living within this natural order is to subject ourselves to fate. The fatalism that results is not about giving up, or submitting to the negative potential for doom. Rather it is based on the realization that it makes no sense to go against the natural order. This fatalism also entails responsibility. Responsibility requires that we act in accordance with natural principles.

The deontology of responsibility we suggest here is consequential, however, in a very complex way. By doing as we should, our rewards are not immediate, or even tangible in the strict sense. Living well, that is, living within this order, is its own reward. Living out of balance with nature has negative implications. Again, we need not experience these implications directly, but they are real, and they are what we might mutually consider as bad, so long as we consider existence as better than non-existence.

The presence of existential risk is a sign of nature's superiority and control over us, and not vice versa. That means to get along with this wider nature we need to know how to deal with risk. Risk is a fact of life. When learning opportunities present the ability to reduce risk in meaningful ways, we take them. When we can't overcome the risks we need to learn to live with them. When the potential risks are large, or catastrophic in nature (i.e., threaten our existence within nature), then we need to act to avoid them. Nature itself has seen fit to give us the intuitive sense to avoid risks that present existential challenges. As we will argue below, this intuition is responsible for a rather remarkable streak of evolutionary survival. To try to go against this intuition is to risk everything. If we do, consciously, the question then becomes, for what? What *value* do we gain in return? The notion of value is therefore key to our conception of deontology, of what ought to be. It is likely that value too is a natural proposition. We value ultimately what conforms with nature, and what assures our proper place in it. In keeping with the theme of complexity in nature, this valuation process is not straightforward. Deontologists of all persuasions are right to denounce any form of value based strictly on utilitarianism, or at least the simple utilitarianism based on physical pleasure and pain. It is not about immediate rewards. The reward we gain goes beyond physical action, and reaction. It is valuable, but not in strictly material terms. We cannot rightly ignore all outcomes, as existence at least is what it is all about.

No doubt we use the jargon of philosophy somewhat loosely here. We do so, however, in the hope that it will promote deeper thinking about risk and how it fits into the wider scheme of life. As the whole concept of a philosophy of risk has received relatively little attention, we would consider these pioneering efforts to meld the language of philosophy with that of the assessment and management of risk somewhat tentative. That is, a cogent philosophy of risk needs to be further developed.

1.3   Why uncertainty is important

As if the issues of our existence were not complicated enough, the real world of risk exists under considerable uncertainty. This uncertainty goes beyond the randomness that underlies probability estimates, to the form that follows from imperfections in our knowledge. We just don't know, and can't know, that much about the world of high-stakes risk and how it will affect us. This uncertainty is, in turn, driven by the complexity and dynamics of the systems that support our existence. We could reasonably infer then, as we make these systems more complex, the uncertainties will increase. Our commitment then has to be to understand these systems as best we can, while at the same time taking proper care that these uncertainties don't exceed our ability to somehow deal them, or at least live in harmony with them.

When the prospects for our existence are so uncertain, it makes sense to try to do things that make them more certain. This is where risk management comes in. In a complex, ever-changing environment, risk management has to be about more than just preventing risk and assuring survival. We can never achieve those guarantees. Risk management is about eliminating worry. This can be achieved either by eliminating risk or by taking actions which we deem satisfactory in the sense we have done all we can. And that means harmonizing risk management with the natural world order.

The proper place of risk management then is to assure that our moral obligations are fulfilled, despite the fact that chance and uncertainty cloud the issue. In fact, chance and uncertainty become part of the issue. Morality takes on the added light of proper attention to the uncertainties involved. Are we adequately identifying, and handling, these uncertainties? When we perceive that these duties are carried out imperfectly, or unequally, they will cause great concern among those possibly effected (which, in the case of high-stakes risk, could be all of us). Uncertainty matters because treating uncertainty improperly carries with it risks of its own. The added dimension of high-stakes risk management is that the very act entails moral obligations.

1.4   The influence of self-interest

To what extent does self-interest, the desire to do better for ourselves, influence the ultimate system by which we live our lives with respect to society or otherwise? In other words, what is the rightful place of self-interest in an ideology of social life? Utilitarianism often takes the individual as its root. Can consequentialism serve the wider community, as well as the wider natural community? The reason for a more widely consequential approach, the mixing of some degree of teleology, or purpose with a purely deontological approach, is to circumvent claims, made by utilitarian philosophers from Jeremy Bentham on down, that deontology and its moral absolutes are simply disguised subjectivities, heavily driven by subjective ideology – what we *feel* is right. Social pronouncements, on risk policy or anything else, therefore become merely a form of ethical and moral elitism: It is so because we know better. The moralist's position in this regard becomes just another form of self-interest. Simple self-interest, however, is not a proper basis for a theory of morals. While self-interest is an essential component of the individual's survival, to the extent it turns *selfish*, or merely self-centered, it can jeopardize that very survival. The system of existence stands, or falls, on how well we all work together within this system. To the extent interdependence makes a difference, whether it is interdependence with our fellow human beings, or the wider natural ecology, we need to temper our self-interest.

It is not about how we value, but what we value. If what we value is determined solely by selfish means, the results will be selfish as well. And there is no guarantee that selfish ends coincide with natural ones. So while economists since Adam Smith have argued that the self-interest of humans is in the best interest of all, including nature, the idea has not withstood the test of time, or at least has done so only very poorly. Empirically, the idea that self-interest promotes the wider interest is, in the language of science, a disproved hypothesis. Those that cling to it so vehemently still are those who benefit most from it – and, then, only at the expense of others.

Attempts to force utilitarian compliance into more self-focused ideologies are widespread. The use of misleading cost/benefit assessments in the high-stakes risk domain is an attempt to push risk acceptance into a framework in which utility valuations are easily manipulated to suit individual interests. The underlying intent is that these situations promote *privileged* progress. More crudely, but accurately, it's a matter of the rich getting richer, while the poor get poorer. It is a philosophy of existence based on, in a word, greed.

On the other hand, the idea of a completely subjective risk ethic falls prey to the criticisms of the utilitarians, based on an intellectual elitism. In these cases, criticism of our ability to understand high-stakes risk goes too far the other way. We can't ever really know the risks we face, so why try? The alternative is some form of pure moral thought, boosted by the notion that this is the way life *should* be lived – and unsupported by evidence from the wider natural whole.

A hallmark of what we might call the moralist strategies with respect to risk is that the pathways to betterment are often left unspecified. The need for "transitions" to a better life is noted, yet without substantive guidance. Presumably, these transitions are supported by our sudden recognition of the value of a path to sustainable, equitable, and risk-free progress – tantamount to a religious conversion, if you will. The problem is that the link to value here is weak, or non-existent. What is it we value, and why? The moralist's position is based on emotions, including desire and longing, backed

by a perceived moral rightness. The root of these perceptions is never well articulated, presumed to be merely
and ultimately "deontological". The need to take some
other path, or abandon the status quo for that matter, is
never made convincing except to those who are already
convinced, based on their own shared ideas about the
matter.

A moral philosophy of risk based on purpose provides at once our psychological impetus, based on moral
sense or intuition, as well as guidelines for achieving purpose. Purpose entails goals, and goals cannot be achieved
without trying. This purposive aspect follows from articulated goals and, in turn, requires an explicit planning
process. We go from a deeper understanding of what
survival means and how we achieve it in a natural setting (based on the technical aspects of risk), to trying to
achieve these goals.

1.5   Rethinking our approach to risk

The groundwork we attempt to set here is designed
around a strongly scientific notion of high-stakes risk.
The power of science, or reason, is our most valuable
human asset in the natural world. However, this science must recognize that what we don't know can be
as important as what we do know. The approach also
recognizes that we can attempt to deal with the at least
partially known nature of risk, albeit at some meta-
level. The premise that at least *some* imperfect knowledge exists suggests that we may be able to plan for
a safe, that is, risk-free, future. This last idea, freedom
from risk, is tempered by the fact that life can never
be made completely risk free. Mere existence requires
us to accept some risk. Yet, this acceptable natural risk
level is itself very low. This relatively low level, while
not making some sort of natural annihilation a strict

impossibility (i.e., probability $= 0$) has nonetheless promoted our remarkable streak of survival through time. Very simply then, by interfering with nature, we jeopardize continued existence.

Appreciating this underlying sense of natural purpose, and the place of existential risk within this purpose, is at the root of what we would call the *radical rethinking* of risk and its relation to progress. By radical we do not imply that it is simply a matter of dramatic change from the status quo. Rather, we look at this radicalism as a way to incorporate a very fundamental way of thinking into everything we do – forever. Radical rethinking is not just about adjusting the way we think about risk; it is about taking ultimate and ultimately very strong action to lead a life in natural harmony. The result is a life in which risks are maintained at some natural level. The approach is radical not in terms of relative change, but in the very basic quality of this change. It is a change that identifies proper thinking with a natural power, very little of which it seems is, or can be, completely known to us. Our approach to risk, therefore, must be shaped by the resulting uncertainty. This is, as we will see, embodied in what we call the precautionary approach to risk. The radicalness of this approach, in turn, lies in its very basic character.

Key to maintaining this basic approach is identifying the level of conviction necessary to achieve the goal of natural risk freedom. This is where the idea of value enters once again. What is really important to us? Value, we would argue, is bound up in the whole notion of living a life in natural harmony. Value is achieved by living harmoniously within the natural world. This naturalness, in turn, is not one of simple physical nature, but suggests a deeper order. This argument is tied to the notion of fate, a representative force of nature to which we must inevitably (by both logical and empirical argument) succumb. The notion of value expressed here is intimately and inexorably tied to the idea of fate. The deontology of existence under this theory owes a lot to the ancient Stoic philosophers. They, uniquely it would seem, understood the deeper notion of a natural order and the importance of adhering to it. To this end, they carefully intertwined the notion of fate with the wider cosmos.

Of Western origin, the ideas of Stoicism are echoed in Eastern philosophy as well, especially Taoism. As the contemporary philosopher C. S. Lewis noted, the idea of a natural order permeates many world philosophies, and religions. The idea underlies especially those religions that find reward in our earthly existence, not beyond it. Our survival then depends on finding "the way"; the path of greatest harmony with nature (i.e., the cosmos).

Radical rethinking contrasts with both the purely utilitarian approach and a strictly deontological moralism. Utilitarians base their consideration solely on the observable here and now. As we have noted, it is dangerous to do so when the here and now is pervaded with so many unknowns. More often than not, this philosophy of living in the observable present is used to promote the ideology of the status quo. To the extent that satisfaction enters the equation, it is usually about the satisfaction of the privileged few versus the many. On the other hand, the moralists push yet another ideology. Their focus is on convincing human beings to behave as they see as "right". The transparency of right behavior, while intuitive, may not be as obvious as the moralists might have us believe. We need at least some element of consequentialism to ground our deontological views. That means going beyond the subjective to the complex, and therefore the more hard to fully understand. Otherwise, we risk arguing that *our* position is right, just because *we* hold it.

The responses radical rethinkers of our path of progress suggest are conditioned by an intuitive view of risk, where intuition is defined here not as some mystical, a priori knowledge, but rather as hard-to-articulate experience. Our human understanding and responses to risk are therefore naturally conditioned, as they are in all living species. Like our other capabilities, so have our responses to risk been honed through evolution. How much we acquire from experience, and how much is ingrained or imprinted at birth is debatable, and certainly an interesting question for further research. This intuitive view of risk also raises the question of how other organic species on the earth today respond to risk. There are likely considerable lessons to be learned about managing high-stakes risk from our earth-mates, many of them whose history on this planet is far longer than humankind's. We outline the basic principles of this intuitive approach to risk in Appendix A. All of these principles are consistent with the approach that considers risk a wider part of nature, to be accommodated, not defeated.

Morality, with regard to this rethinking of risk, is what is natural, in the sense of preserving the natural system which we inhabit. What separates the radical rethinker from the moralist is this view of value as preserving the cosmic order. Our transitions are, in turn, guided by this *telos*, or purpose. The problem is, of course, that we might not be able to truly know how the wider system works, just as the ancient Stoics thought the mind of God, or creation, to be fundamentally unknowable. The search becomes one for signals, however weak, on how we might live a life more concordant with this natural evolution. The moral approach is in this way given a sense of purpose beyond the merely subjective. The ideology, then, of the radical rethinker becomes an ideology of purpose based on natural order. That, in turn, requires a commitment to some natural level of risk.

How prepared we are, as individuals, business organizations, communities, and as a society in general, to make such commitments is another matter. Values matter, but values can be obscured and otherwise conflict. Unfortunately, a wait-and-see attitude is not acceptable when existence is at stake. We need to commit to a process of risk management "up front" and stick with it. This commitment, and what it entails in terms of real effects on our lives, is what gives us considerable consternation about making existential decisions about risk.

Yet if everything is a matter of fate, why do anything – radical or otherwise? For guidance on this quandary, we turn once again to the knowledge of the Stoics. In their theory of the cosmic order of things, they held that responsibility of action is completely compatible with the idea of fate. Living the natural life is then tantamount to living responsibly. If we are sick, why see a doctor? Why not let nature (fate) just take its course? The answer lies in the fact that seeing a doctor and survival are *co-fated* events. If you are to survive through medical treatment, then it is your related fate to see a doctor. The Stoics also believed that nature imbues certain characteristics on the things that occupy the world, including humans. Just as a cylinder has innate properties which cause it to roll in a different pattern when pushed down a hill than, say, a cone-shaped object. The path these objects take when pushed is in effect fated, yet determined by their inherent characteristics. In the same way, a Stoic would argue, our paths through life are influenced by our character. To build this character as a reflection of the cosmic order is what underlies the notion of the natural life, or living within nature. We would argue that living the natural life also entails living life within the risk boundaries set by natural events.

1.6   The need to plan

Applying the theory of risk management to survival entails the natural notions of planning (setting the means to achieve goals) and control (making sure plans work as desired). This is how our moral commitments come to fruition – by action, not wishful thinking. We consider planning to be natural because all organisms on the earth are regulated by a purposive process: "Organism" implies *organization*. The successive steps of evolution toward some goal, then, is what we might rightfully identify as the most basic form of planning.

The existence of this regulative process, striving toward some goal, or goals, is what separates a purposive world from some indeterminate, or completely random, one. Though we may not fully understand this purpose, according to the notion of an underlying *telos*, we need to heed what imperfect signals we can discern. Only in this way can we gain some reasonable comfort that we are at least heading in the right direction.

A radical rethinking of our approach to risk means that change must begin at its core. This does not mean the individual, but rather the social system and institutions that shape the individual's thinking. This is why planning must itself be achieved at the social and institutional level. Only in this way can we hope to harmonize social progress with the natural scheme of things. As we complicate the world for the sake of progress, we need to take natural risk levels into account, and adjust accordingly. This approach recognizes the compatibility of responsibility and fate.

We could, of course, decide to return to a more primitive state, in which case planning, while not abandoned, at least becomes less formal. Responding to this raw state becomes simply a matter of evolution. To the extent we choose to pursue goals beyond mere subsistence – the search for progress – we then need to make the planning process more deliberate. Planning and progress in this sense go together.

It is likely that more deliberate planning is itself merely a step in the evolution of humans within this wider natural setting. It is a move toward the realization of a perfection, a utopia if you will, in which natural harmony means that deliberate planning and control themselves eventually become perfunctory. Progress and harmony with nature then become one. Our current phase can thus be viewed as one of development and adjustment toward this more perfect state. It remains, however, a matter of properly recognizing and acting on our responsibilities to the deeper world order. In effect, planning is helping us to learn to live in conformity with this order, while achieving the wider benefits of progress. The complexity of the problem is magnified by the many interests involved. Progress is achieved collectively. It is due to this large scale that we need some guidelines, perhaps even some technical help, for achieving the right balance.

Risk planning, in conjunction with other social and economic planning structures, must not therefore be viewed as some unnatural or forced process. Rather, it is a way to make plain our underlying assumptions about goals and how we feel we can best achieve these goals to maintain an essentially worry free life. To the extent planning is perceived to, or may actually, impinge on anyone's sense of freedom or free will is up to the individual. We have to be very careful, however, that we don't let our individual views negatively impact the survival of the whole. Certain selfish tendencies may be part of human nature. It is then part of the planning process to try to overcome these. To the extent these tendencies become resistant to coordination, then there is nothing we can really do to really fix things.

1.7   A note on the meaning of *survival*

High-stakes risks are important because they threaten our very survival. We use the notion of survival here in a sense wider than the literal notion. In fact, it seems extremely unlikely that humankind, or life on earth in general, can be completely extinguished by any theoretically controllable, predominantly human-made, means. This presents a counter-argument to the finality of any risk, as long as a single human, or cell, for that matter, remains. This improbable, though possible, outcome would seem to counteract the worst risk we could throw at it. So rather than complete extinction, we also include conditions under which life is simply not worth living. These may be physical conditions, which result in a severe deterioration of health, yet do not preclude physical survival of the organism as a living being. They also include, perhaps more controversially, psychological conditions. These psychological conditions, however, would be deemed severe, such as arising from severe psychosis or depression. They may likely have physical repercussions as well, as many psychoses do. They might also lead to physical issues of existence on a social scale, to the extent living conditions promote crime, violence, and warfare. These potential outcomes would seem, while qualitatively as bad as extinction, much more likely in any reasonable risk scenario, especially those that might be human-made.

As we have pointed out in the section on uncertainty, above, the complexity with which the conditions of survival intertwine makes the uncertainty about our existence especially significant. First of all, the mental condition of living under growing uncertainties about our existence can affect our mental survival, or at least the achievement of a suitable quality of life the reasonable person would consider worth surviving. Beyond the mental aspects, uncertainty may itself create technological and social responses that can increase the possibility of disaster. When uncertainty creates panic, or despair, these psychological conditions may manifest themselves physically, as in the case of social unrest and even warfare. A desperate search for solutions in technology may also act to increase uncertainty, as these actions may have further unknown counter-effects.

Survival then is not only about the ends, but also about the means of our journey through life. Obviously, survival is a necessary condition for enjoyment of life, but in and of itself, it is not sufficient. The synergy of purpose we ultimately look for in achieving natural ways to achieve survival is to do so while maintaining the highest degree of happiness, or satisfaction, possible. This does not make the process utilitarian or hedonistic in and of itself. It is important to recognize that the process is not driven simply by these goals, but rather happiness becomes a natural byproduct of doing the right thing, with respect to our own survival, that of others.

The deontology of survival, what we *ought* to do to achieve survival, in this wider sense of satisfying survival we have developed here, is therefore a idea that cannot be understood in isolation from outcomes, in a wider, cosmic sense. Nor can it be divorced from value. The whole philosophy of high-stakes risk is intertwined, without being circular. We value survival, but not in terms of survival itself. That should be very clear from the way humans approach the idea of existence. Survival has to be woven into a wider tapestry that represents living life in accordance with nature (i.e., the wider cosmic purpose, or *telos*). The payoff is not just survival, but survival along with the satisfaction of fitting into the bigger picture. This satisfaction is not itself simply subjective, or peculiar to the individual, but objective in the sense that natural order provides us with the good life – both satisfying and continuous.

A comment is in order here as well on the notion of survival in the context of a physical nature beyond human existence. Physical nature is all part of what we consider the wider natural cosmos, and therefore subject to the idea of teleology or purpose. Undoubtedly, this purpose is intertwined among human and non-human life. On this basis alone, we have good reason to suspect that our survival depends in many ways on the survival of physical nature as a whole. This point is made clear in the work of so-called *deep ecologists*, who study and emphasize the interdependent nature of human and non-human existence. Deep ecology, despite being obviously and necessarily a human endeavor, is nonetheless concerned more about preserving the survival of nature itself, independent of the human's place in it. This factor tends to make it somewhat controversial in general, aside from its relatively uncontroversial technical points on the interdependence of all life. The ideas about survival promoted here, especially the notion of a wider cosmic order that includes all life, is in tune with the concerns of deep ecology about making the world more survivable by all inhabitants, not just humans. We stop short, however, of advocating a risk management for this whole natural world, in and of itself. By not adopting this wider view we do not mean to promote an explicitly human-centered approach. Rather, our choice to focus discussion on human beings is based on a conviction that the wider cosmos will provide for the survival of the natural world as part of its overall purpose, or fate. To take survival in its widest sense and apply it to physical nature in general, we might just say that the approach here recognizes that the wider natural world has existed before humans, and will most likely exist after them. That the current destruction of parts of the non-human natural world is to be decried on a variety of moral and practical grounds is no doubt true. However, we will be concerned here primarily with those that affects humans, and tangentially, the wider natural world because humans are (obviously) our exclusive audience. While human beings have the ability to do something about their existence, they are at the same time the creatures in this world that most need to. Perhaps the two are interrelated. Given at least the possibility that the human race may be bound for a not so happy ending, we also express our solidarity with deep ecology in hoping that whatever collateral damage to the natural environment it does along the way will ultimately be survivable by the natural planet it leaves behind.

Further reading

The notion of natural laws that underlie most faiths of the world is outlined in C. S. Lewis' *The Abolition of Man* (Macmillan, 1947). There Lewis notes that it is humankind's duty to live within this natural law, or risk extinction.

The Stoic's notions of fate and determinism are explored in Susan Bobzien's *Determinism and Freedom in Stoic Philosophy* (Oxford University Press, 1998). For a more general treatment of the influential philosophy of the Stoics, see *The Stoics* (Hackett Publishing, 1994), by F. H. Sandbach.

The various theories of moral commitments are explored in James Rachels' *Elements of Moral Philosophy* (McGraw-Hill, 2002). See also *Ethics* (Prentice Hall, 1973), by William Frankena.

Immanuel Kant's outline of moral philosophy of absolutes appears in his *Grounding for a Metaphysics of Morals* (Hackett

Publishing, 1993), originally published in 1785. For a modern application of Kant's philosophy of morals within the framework of environmental risks, see John Martin Gillroy's *Justice & Nature: Kantian Philosophy, Environmental Policy, and the Law* (Georgetown University Press, 2001). Gillroy suggests Kant's philosophy of responsibility supports what he calls the *environmental imperative* which is to "harmonize humanity and nature!"

The modern utilitarian position was articulated in the work of John Stuart Mill, see especially *Utilitarianism* (Hackett, 2002), a pamphlet originally published in 1863. For an ends-directed perspective on Kant's moral philosophy, which reconciles (somewhat) deontological and utilitarian views, see *Kantian Conseqeuntialism* (Oxford University Press, 1996), by David Cummiskey.

Planning experts have long recognized the relationship between planning and natural systems. Rexford G. Tugwell – scholar, statesman, conservationist, and architect of many aspects of planning in Roosevelt's "New Deal" – wrote: "Everyone who really goes to work at 'planning' is forced eventually to realize that what he is trying to bring about is a state of nature" ("Earthbound: The Problem of Planning and Survival", *The Antioch Review*, Winter, 1949). See also Melville Branch, *Planning: Universal Process* (Praeger, 1990).

On the basic tenets of deep ecology, and their relation to human survival, see *Deep Ecology: Living as if Nature Mattered* (Gibbs Smith, 2001), by Bill Devall and George Sessions.

2
Making Decisions Under Conditions of Risk

While the risks of life tend to raise concerns, they are often expressed only vaguely. It would seem that many of us rely on the ability of scientists, regulators, politicians, and business people to understand the nature of these risks, and act in the best interest of all that may be exposed to them. Although our concerns may be serious, many of us feel that those that can really do anything about these risks are able to understand, and hence control them. After all, that's what a comprehensive plan of risk management at the individual, business or social level is all about, isn't it?

Risk, however, is not a characteristic of the world which can be treated uniformly throughout its spectrum of impacts. While we can rely on a well-developed theory of statistics to handle many risks, these simple applications can fail us when risks are at their most potent. To manage high-stakes risks – those that may affect our very existence – we need to understand the unique character of these risks.

2.1 The nature of chance events

The basic concept of risk is simple. <u>Risk is associated with the *probability* of untoward event</u>s. Probability represents that form of uncertainty due to <u>*randomness*</u>. Randomness arises from our inability to specify the exact conditions under which an experiment, action or event occurs." As a result, the outcomes of the process are subject to variation. To illustrate the idea of randomness, consider a bowl filled with colored balls (Figure 2.1). We mix the bowl well, and draw without looking. We cannot be sure of which color ball will appear on the next draw, yet we *can* identify the *long run* outcome in terms of averages. This is due to the fact that at least some conditions influencing the outcomes are known (in this case, that we have a mixed bowl of various colored balls). We also often make the assumption that this mix remains unchanged during the experiment.

This long run average property of random events is what we refer to as its probability. The probability that some event *x* will occur, $P(x)$, can be expressed using the simple ratio,

$$P(x) = \frac{\text{Number of outcomes in which x occurs}}{\text{Total number of outcomes}}$$

In our urn example, let's say the event of interest is drawing a black ball. Of the ten balls in the urn, only one

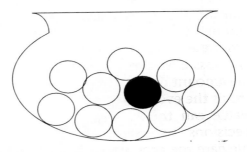

Figure 2.1   The "urn model" of probability

is black. Applying the probability equation we calculate the probability of drawing a black ball as 1/10, or .1. If we repeatedly draw balls from the urn, the black ball will come up, on average, once every ten draws. Even without knowing the composition of the bowl ahead of time, we could infer it by repeated draws, in a process known as *statistical sampling*.

Probabilities are often calculated over some period of time, rather than as individual draws. For example, we may predict through statistical observation that a major snowstorm occurs once every five years in our region. Outcomes in this case are associated with a time period of a year. Observing one outcome of interest (a major storm) once every five years suggests a probability of 1/5, or .2. We could express this probability by saying the *annual* probability of a major snowstorm is "one-in-five".

In the field of risk, we may consider drawing the black ball as resulting in the occurrence of some untoward event, entailing some loss, or reduction of value over a fixed period of time (usually a year). Drawing a black ball now corresponds to the loss event, while a draw of white means no loss. In this way, the simple urn draw could be used to model the real-world event. Through repeated observations of the real world (i.e., statistical sampling) we establish the annual probability of any loss event. We could also compute a degree of confidence based on other possible sample outcomes, based on the axioms of statistical modeling.

When a monetary or other identifiable value is associated with a loss event, we can use the probability to calculate the amount of loss over time. This average loss is referred to as the event's *expected value* over time. The expected value can then be used to make important financial decisions. For example, insurance companies can help alleviate the problem of financial risk by pooling risk statistics among their policy holders, and pricing instruments of indemnification ("insurance policies") accordingly. These prices, or *premiums*, can be conveniently and relatively accurately adjusted over time as the average loss for an insured exposure manifests itself. Likewise, an employer can institute safety programs based on statistical observation of workplace injuries, the cost effectiveness of any such programs established over the relatively short term, as statistics become available.

On a wider scale, community public safety programs against crime can be adjusted based on observed outcomes of protection and prevention plans. In such cost/benefit decisions, we simply substitute the average, or expected, value of loss for some exact value of costs, and weigh it against benefits (whose value might also be statistically derived). The comfort we gain from such calculations is that our outcomes (e.g., gain over cost) will manifest themselves over a fairly observable timeframe, depending on the statistical properties of the risk.

Key to the statistical analysis of risk is the ability to identify the probabilistic characteristics of an event. To do so, we need to be able to observe some reasonable series of these events in time (i.e., take an adequate sample). Difficulties arise when statistical data gets scarce, as it inevitably does when the impacts of risk get large enough. We are now faced with an urn in which the occurrence of the black ("loss") ball may be very rare, yet not impossible. How do we assess the possibilities, and properly account for them in these cases? Perhaps more significantly, can the resulting probabilities serve as a reliable measure of the long-run costs and benefits associated with the treatment of such risks?

2.2   High-stakes decisions are *unique*

In the real world, the assessment of probabilities is rarely as simple as judging the likelihood of draws from an urn. Probability estimation, especially for rare, complex events, is difficult to do with any degree of precision simply because the events are so infrequent. The properties generating these probabilities are complex, and may themselves change over time. In terms of our urn example, we may not know if the composition of the urn (the number of balls of various colors) is itself changing over repeated draws. The dynamics and complexity of real-world sampling means that we face a type of uncertainty *beyond* randomness. The type of uncertainty that enters is very different from chance, or randomness, reflected in the variability of results over time. This other form of uncertainty is rather a reflection of the genuinely *unknown*.

When we don't know some property for sure, due to imperfect knowledge, the best we can do is assess some *interval*, or set, of possibilities. When we have complete knowledge of some property, say, the number of sides in a triangle, we express that knowledge precisely: A triangle has *three* sides. Complete uncertainty, on the other hand, would be represented by an interval that includes all possibilities – nothing is excluded. Usually, our knowledge supports some degree of possibility between precision and complete ignorance. We might, as in the case of the outdoor temperature tomorrow, assess some rough interval of possibilities. Given the information at hand, we might believe that tomorrow's temperature will be between 30 and 50 degrees Fahrenheit. Alternatively, such uncertainties are often expressed in linguistic expressions that roughly represent this interval: We think it will be *cool* tomorrow.

Note once again that the uncertainty expressed here is different from randomness. We are not talking about the probability that the temperature tomorrow will fall somewhere in the range between 30 and 50 degrees, only that it might *possibly* fall anywhere in between.

This result does not depend on the variability of results over time, as when we assume the conditions are right to apply the statistical model. It is due to our inability to understand the details of weather dynamics enough to be able to determine tomorrow's temperature with any degree of precision. Whereas statistical results depend on outcomes which are revealed over some longer term (the statistical average), uncertainty due to knowledge imperfection applies to our knowledge (or, perhaps, lack of knowledge) about the single event at hand – tomorrow's temperature and the complex weather dynamics that determine it. It can only be reduced by finding new information on how the system under study works, and not simply by repeated trials. Inherent complexity means that uncertainties due to knowledge imperfection may in some cases *never* be resolved, introducing at least some element of *indeterminacy*.

While randomness and knowledge imperfection are different forms of uncertainty, they can occur together. When we have good knowledge of the underlying process of sampling, say the toss of a fair coin, or a draw from an urn whose basic composition is known (or can be inferred by repeated draws), we an use precise probabilities to express long-run outcomes. When we have no idea of the underlying structure, perhaps because we suspect that structure is changing, or otherwise complicated, or repeated draws are simply not available to us, we need to use rough estimates based on available knowledge. We often express such imperfectly known probabilities using words, such as "probable", or "unlikely" or "rare". These words, rather than expressing a precise single probability that the event may occur within some specified number of trials, say for example, one chance in a thousand, or .001, express a *range* of probabilities, consistent with the evidence at hand. So, the annual probability of an earthquake in a relatively seismically inactive area may be deemed by the experts as "unlikely". A more formal representation may suggest a best guess of one-in-one thousand (.001), but include this in a range of uncertainty that may run from, say, one-in-five hundred (.002) on the high end to one-in-five thousand (.0002) on the low end. This interval estimate expresses our uncertainty due to knowledge imperfection about the uncertainty due to randomness.

Risk analysts express uncertainties due to knowledge imperfection in a variety of ways. The simplest is using simple intervals, as shown above. Intervals can be used to identify the uncertainty about probability, impact, or both, when it comes to risky events. These intervals, usually formed around some single best guess estimate, show the bounds of possibility (*not* probability) around the best guess. In creating these intervals, the analyst determines the widest range the probabilities and impacts can take, given the information available. The proper interval is not determined directly from data, as in the case of statistical estimates of sampling uncertainty, but rather *instrumentally*. That is, we judge the appropriate interval by how well it lets us reason about a world where our knowledge is imperfect. So, in estimating how many tennis balls may fit into a shoe box, what we know about the physical restrictions may suggest that from eight to twelve may fit (defining an *interval of possibility*). Our estimates in this case are guided by rough application of physical laws, and experience. How well they let us deal with the world influences our future estimates in similar uncertain situations.

In many cases, how exact our statements are determine how useful they may be in achieving some goal. The more precise our statements about something which we only have very imperfect knowledge about, the less possible it will contain the true value. Setting the appropriate interval, therefore, always entails the tradeoff between specificity, or exactness, and truth. It is crucial to recognize, however, that the degree of uncertainty contains important information in and of itself. Not knowing exactly what the temperature will be out tomorrow, for whatever reason, may determine our choice of dress, activity, and so on.

In assessing the impacts of the risks we face in life, knowledge imperfection means that we can only identify ranges of outcomes. In Figure 2.2, we show the various ranges of probability estimates associated with a universe in which losses range from inconsequential to catastrophic (bounded, theoretically at least, by infinite (∞) loss). The rectangles around the point estimates show our uncertainty about where the true probability and impact may fall. As we often experience in life, the larger the impact, the lower the likelihood and, as a result, the more uncertainty about the estimate (due to data scarcity). As it turns out, our ability to identify probabilities starts to fail us at the point we need it

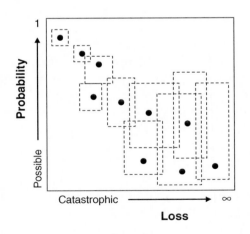

Figure 2.2 Imperfectly known probabilities complicate high-stakes risk analysis

most – when losses are the largest. Nonetheless, as in the case of weather predictions, even imperfect estimates can provide valuable guidance on how we manage these high-stakes risks.

We could also extend the analysis of uncertainty due to knowledge imperfection using intervals graded by confidence, or relative possibility. This type of expression of uncertainty is known as *fuzziness*, and can be defined by a simple distribution of graded outcomes. In our temperature example, we might feel that our estimate of outdoor temperature tomorrow may encompass the range from 30 to 50 degrees, with 40 degrees as our "best guess". This information defines a fuzzy range of values, with 40 degree being the most possible, and the relative possibilities tailing off in both directions. Once again, the shape of these fuzzy possibility functions is determined instrumentally, and not directly from data. And as in the case of intervals, fuzzy functions need not be defined precisely to be useful.

2.3   Facing the *catastrophe problem*

Uncertainty due to knowledge imperfection can be incorporated into the statistical decision process. For example, rather than calculate expected value based on some single, best guess estimate, we can include values computed using the end-points of the interval. This gives us a built-in measure of the potential variability of our outcomes, due to knowledge imperfection. We need not necessarily abandon the averaging process due to knowledge imperfection alone. Perhaps the most significant complicating feature of high-stakes risks, however, is their *finality*. In the arena of catastrophe, we don't get a second chance to get things right. That is, with catastrophic events, the fundamental problem is that *in the long run, there may be no long run*. That means that reliance on statistical averages that manifest themselves over time is *not an option*, regardless of how well we might be able to specify the likelihood of these events.

Experience can, of course, provide us with some important guidelines, but we cannot hope to manage rare yet catastrophic events in the same way we do more frequent, low impact losses. Yet it is precisely in the management of existential risk that the stakes are so high. It behooves us, therefore, to put our understanding of high-stakes risks, and what we can do to manage them, on a sounder footing.

The basic challenge we face when confronted with the potential for catastrophe can be easily summarized using a simple graph known as a *decision matrix*. A decision matrix is a chart that shows possible actions, choices, or decisions, on one axis, and potential "states of the world" on another. The intersection of choice and state of the world shows the possible outcomes of our choices.

The decision matrix shown in Figure 2.3 generalizes decision under conditions of high-stakes (catastrophic) risk. To simplify, we limit ourselves to two actions: Act to

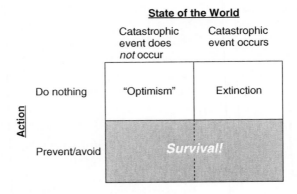

Figure 2.3   Responding to existential risks

avoid the catastrophe, or do nothing. Likewise, the state of the world is represented by a catastrophe occurring, or not. By taking action, we forestall the effects of catastrophe, regardless of the state of the world. In other words, we neutralize the effects of catastrophe, by either removing them at the source (loss prevention) or reducing or eliminating their effects (loss protection). In the process, we assure *survival*. Should we choose to do nothing, and the conditions of catastrophe do not materialize, we lose nothing. In positive terms, we continue to live the "high life", supported only by pure optimism. The suggestion is that this life *potentially* provides maximum satisfaction, or pleasure, on a purely utilitarian basis. We might properly characterize this decision approach as *fatalistic*: We do nothing, and hope for the best. Doing nothing therefore becomes the *least cost outcome*, both in terms of direct costs and foregone opportunities ("opportunity costs").

Avoiding risk is at the root of the *precautionary* approach to high-stakes risks. In more technical terms, precaution amounts to *minimax'ing* in the face of severe loss potentials. Under the minimax decision criterion, we choose that action that minimizes the maximum possible loss, regardless of the likelihood of the various outcomes. In the case of the matrix, that action is choosing to prevent or avoid exposures to potentially catastrophic events. Though precaution based on the minimax is often criticized as being too strict, the fact remains that, just as Kant had specified in his *categorical imperative*, the potential for infinite penalties requires a strong commitment to preventing those outcomes. On this basis, the precautionary concept is becoming more widely used as a principle of both risk regulation and control, and the global legislation of conduct with respect to potential high-stakes risks.

2.4 Fatalism and precaution: The *only* two choices

The analysis of high-stakes risk, with special attention to the catastrophe problem, suggests that there are only two logical responses to high-stakes risk. We can either avoid them (precaution), or ignore them (fatalism). *There is no in-between.* Application of statistical techniques to risks that entail the potential for irreversible losses simply does not make sense (the "catastrophe problem"). To the extent we observe such techniques being applied to high-stakes risks they either are foisted on us in an attempt to foster some self-interested agenda, or are applied in ignorance. More often than not, we choose to overlook these defects, in the false hope that they may help us achieve security without us having to give up too much. Used in this way, statistical approaches merely represent a disguised fatalism which ultimately entails uncritical acceptance of risk. The only difference is that we may be fooled (or fool ourselves) into feeling better about the whole thing.

The need for special tools to deal with extreme risks does not mean that we ignore obvious dangers, including statistical ones. Survival is about tending to the obvious details of life, as well as the more obscure ones. We must recognize, however, that in dealing with statistical risk we are only working with the very tip of the risk iceberg – those risks that manifest themselves within a relatively observable, short-run window. There is no guarantee that anything we do to reduce statistical risk will alleviate the threat that high-stakes risks pose. After all, all it takes is one. The extreme nature of the outcomes in high-stakes decisions forces extreme responses.

It may seem then that the only two feasible decision strategies, precaution and fatalism, are polar opposites. In fact, a reconciliation is not only possible, but critical to the success of high-stakes risk management in a complex world. We might even say that reconciling the two is what risk management is all about. We want to be able to legitimately eliminate worry about disaster. The only way to do so is to work to equate the satisfaction that we are doing everything possible to reduce risk, with the recognition that we can only do so much.

As we will see, the biggest challenge to our survival depends not on which principle to follow, precaution or fatalism, but on how we reconcile the two. In assessing the pathways to survival, the choice of which determines how much we value existence (ours, and that of the world around us), we find that a genuine fatalism, beyond mere acquiescence, is at one with the spirit of precautionary avoidance. When is avoiding risk synonymous with doing nothing? *When avoiding risk becomes part of our natural existence.*

Further reading

For an introduction to the type of uncertainty that underlies probability and statistics, see *Randomness* (Harvard University Press, 1998), by Deborah Bennet. An accessible introduction to the theory of probability is *The Architecture of Chance: An Introduction to the Logic and Arithmetic of Probability* (Oxford University Press, 1989), by Richard Lowry. Edmund C. Berkeley provides a unique introduction to the concrete nature of probability using experiments with physical devices, such as our urn draw, in *Probability and Statistics: An Introduction Through Experiments* (Science Materials Center, 1961).

On how ideas about probability and risk enter the decision-making process, see *Choices: An Introduction to Decision Theory* (University of Minnesota Press, 1987), by Michael Resnik. Resnik includes a good, albeit brief, introduction to precautionary decision criteria (minimax) as well.

Standard texts on decision theory emphasize (indeed, overemphasize) the statistical nature of risk. A powerful, and very practical, treatise on the unique characteristics of decision-making under conditions of high-stakes risk is Stephan Haller's *Apocalypse Soon? Wagering on Warnings of Global Catastrophe* (McGill-Queens University Press, 2002). The philosopher Nicholas Rescher provides a particularly insightful discussion of high-stakes decisions in *Risk: A Philosophical Introduction to the Theory of Risk Evaluation and Management* (University Press of America, 1983).

For a wider view of uncertainty, including the varieties due to knowledge imperfection and their treatment, see Michael Smithson's *Ignorance and Uncertainty* (Springer Verlag, 1989). For more on the extension of the idea of intervals of uncertainty (knowledge imperfection) to include grades of confidence to express the inherent *fuzziness* of complex measurements and concepts, see the collection of seminal papers of fuzzy pioneer Lotfi Zadeh, collected in R. Yager, H. T. Nguyen, R. M. Tong, and S. Ovchinnikov (eds.), *Fuzzy Sets and Applications: Selected Papers of L. A. Zadeh* (Wiley, 1987). A more general introduction is Bart Kosko's *Fuzzy Thinking: The New Science of Fuzzy Logic* (Hyperion, 1993). Both intervals and fuzzy representations (fuzzy *sets* and their associated logic) are used by risk analysts to express the wider uncertainty inherent in real-world probability estimates.

The precautionary approach and its application to wide-scale risk management of catastrophic risks in a variety of domains is discussed in *Protecting Public Health and the Environment: Implementing the Precautionary Principle* (Island Press, 1999), by Caroline Raffensperger and Joel Tickner. See also this author's *Precautionary Risk Management: Dealing with Catastrophic Loss Potentials in Business, the Community and Society* (Palgrave Macmillan, 2006).

3
The Notion of a Naturally Risk-Free Existence

The most effective approach to managing the unique nature of high-stakes risks is to avoid them. This simple rule is what defines the precautionary approach to risk, based on the *minimax* criterion. While avoidance is an unassailable preventative from a theoretical standpoint, a practical issue remains. Striving for a *genuinely* zero level of risk is not just inconvenient, it is impossible. A true zero level of risk cannot exist, by the physical laws of the universe. This does not mean, however, that we have to abandon minimax precaution as a powerful form of risk mitigation. To be effectively precautionary, we need to focus on achieving a level of risk that is compatible with *natural background levels*.

As it turns out, a modified view of possibility, and the degree of reasoned risk acceptance it entails, can provide us with practical guidance in achieving a safer world. This more reasoned look also suggests that precaution need not stand, or fall, on the goal of achieving a strictly zero risk level. In this way, a naturally risk-free world becomes a survivable world which we can achieve *practically*. This view of risk fits in with our view of survival as dependent on maintaining a natural order.

3.1   The challenge of practical precaution

Applying the minimax rule in its strictest sense entails a peculiar result with respect to risk: For the most part, it ignores probabilities. The only likelihood of relevance is that which separates *possibility* from *impossibility*. That is, once we consider a catastrophic event as *possible*, we avoid it. We simply minimize the potential for large possible impacts, regardless of how likely (or unlikely) they are. Generally, this approach requires far less information than being able to define the probability of any degree of loss with precision.

Yet, how do we define *possibility*? A strict definition suggests *any event with greater than zero probability* is possible, in the physical sense. This means that as long as the probability of a catastrophic loss is some positive number, however small, we take action to avoid it. The practical problem we encounter in applying this strict definition of minimax is that the approach suggests that *we should avoid everything, because anything is possible* (i.e., in the strictest sense, every action we take entails risk).

Statistical physics tells us that there is a tiny, yet non-zero, probability that a flat car tire might spontaneously re-inflate. It would certainly be foolish, however, for a stranded motorist to wait for this to happen instead of calling for a tow truck. Nor could we lead our lives under the theoretically possible specter that some black hole will open up on our next step, and engulf us in nothingness. Critics of precaution based on the minimax suggest we abandon the whole idea of strict avoidance of risk for just this reason – it is simply unworkable in practice. However, there is what logic may tell us, and there is what we know to be true, by virtue of that long streak of evolutionary learning that builds our risk *intuition*. This intuition tells us that we can live safely in the world, and that everything is *not* risky. We need to somehow reconcile intuition, and the remarkable streak of evolution which it has supported, with some reasonable definition of what is really risky. Practical application of the minimax therefore rests on a proper definition of what "possibility" means.

3.2 Toward an idea of "natural risk"

While various criteria exist for acceptable (non-zero) risk, we focus here on what may be the most promising, at least from our wider, natural perspective. That level of acceptability is based on the fact that some level of risk has existed since the beginning of existence on life on earth. This background level, or what we may call the *natural risk level*, is consistent with a relatively long streak of evolutionary survival. Though the exact level of natural risk may be difficult to define, nothing suggests that it is *too* difficult, or impossible in principle. Certainly, there exists no reason to not at least investigate the potential for establishing some such level. We may begin, for example, by establishing some relative valuation of the time life has existed on earth between natural cataclysms. In fact, scientists have identified periods for which the earth can survive in relatively unfettered fashion, subject only to genuinely natural, or naturally occurring cataclysms. By identifying such comparisons of potential survivability we can get an impression of how alarmingly high the potential of such man-made threats as global nuclear conflict are. By most indications, an unfettered natural existence may provide millions of years of evolutionary progress. By human-made risk standards, we may be challenged to exist hundreds more.

Not that the idea of a natural risk level is without its challenges. The concept of being "natural" is complex and, as a result, hard to define. Clearly, when we use the term we mean more than physical nature, or what we more usually refer to as our natural environment – trees, water, air, animals, insects, and so on. It is closer to the wider idea of a cosmos or world order. Just where then might we set this level of natural risk? Observers have suggested that these levels may be set somewhere around the proverbial "one in a million" for annual extinction probability of individuals, maybe to one in a hundred thousand or so. Such levels tend to blend with common background levels such as lightning strikes, animal or insect bites, asteroid collisions, and other natural events. Note that these levels roughly represent the inverse of the modern epoch of existence of life on earth.

3.3   Probability, possibility, and *propensity*

It may turn out on further investigation that deeper intuitions underlie the probability measures that define the difference between practical possibility and impossibility. For example, the improbability of a high-stakes event may be linked to the notion of physical complexity. Complex combinations of events are harder to realize, and are therefore more rare. The definition of possibility in this way may hinge on some non-probabilistic measure of system complexity.

We might in fact merge the frequency notion of probability (as represented by drawing colored balls from an urn or bowl) with complexity using the so-called *propensity interpretation* of probability. Propensity interpretations attempt to overcome the logical difficulties associated with applying the long-run frequency definition to the single case. What does it really mean that the toss of this particular coin will land heads with a probability of .5? While we might expect the series of tosses to average out at 1/2, or .5, the single case either lands heads or it doesn't. Yet, we often make at least intuitive judgments about what will happen on the next individual toss of a die, or at least adjust our decisions according to such apparent single cases. And then there is also the issue of non-repeatable, or unique, events. Last, but not least, is our issue in which the next toss of a coin may be our last (probabilistic survival). The propensity definition of probability suggests that these random outcomes are nonetheless influenced by the physical properties of the event. For example, the outcome of a coin toss depends on the physical properties of a coin, most notably the symmetry of the two sides. As these properties exist in the coin itself, the propensity they represent, for example, the behavior of the coin when tossed, is reflected in a single event.

It makes sense that rarity itself stems from some physical properties of an event or action. It may be perhaps something that makes the event less susceptible to occurrence. We often attempt to influence the safety of some act or event by actively trying to retard its occurrence, as when we install sprinkler protection against fires in a building. The fact remains, however, that we can only verify the outcomes of such actions experimentally. Leaving open the question of a deeper definition of possibility of occurrence of risk events, we will continue for now to treat the distinction between possible and impossible in terms of the frequency definition of probability.

3.4 Risk, subsistence, and *safe* progress

Setting natural levels of risk does not mean that only the forces of nature can conform to them. Indeed, in the sense that human activities can achieve comparable natural levels they may become indistinguishable, at least by our definition. The difference is that with human-induced risks, achieving natural risk levels may be somewhat within our control. This element of control is what gives humans the ability to direct their progress while maintaining natural risk levels. To some degree at least, we can take our evolution into our own hands. To do so, however, demands respect for those deeper evolutionary forces which control the wider cosmos of which humans are a (very) small part.

The philosophical question, and one of ultimately very practical value, is if we can achieve *at least* some degree of subsistence at this most very basic level of natural risk. If so, progress can be measured by how far we get beyond subsistence *safely*. At its most basic level, this requires setting some standard in terms of natural activities. The *subsistence level* of risk becomes that natural level at which basic life, including health and a reasonable degree of happiness, is supported.

The proper goal of science, then, is moving us beyond subsistence. As a result, the idea of planning with respect to subsistence levels does not *necessarily* commit us, as some critics might suggest, to a primitive life. That said, there remains the possibility that safety *may* ultimately require some reconsideration of the level of comfort we achieve *vis-à-vis* survival. Some observers argue that in a return to a safe level of existence, some level of primitivism is unavoidable. The counterargument is that such primitivism would in fact increase risk levels, not reduce them. This argument, however, presumes its conclusion. Any degree of safety presumes some baseline. To argue that safety can never be achieved is to undermine the process of risk management itself. Otherwise, why bother? That this baseline should be sought in a world untouched by human action seems like a reasonable starting point. As we have noted above, this stance does not commit us to a position of zero risk. Nor does primitivism commit us to complete acceptance of some positive level of risk without attempts to reduce that risk, even if it is natural. Humankind even in its most primitive existence sought to avoid natural dangers. We built shelters, we fashioned protective clothing, we banded together against the threat of various natural perils, we sought to increase the level of hygiene and resistance to disease, we armed ourselves against natural predators, and so on. Once again, survival may reduce to simply doing what comes naturally.

To maintain the hope of survival we need to believe that at least some safe haven against risk exists. There has to be somewhere that we could reach to assure some minimum promise of survival. Suggesting that no such place exists is to extinguish this hope. Practically, to suggest that this safe haven can only be achieved by further progress is based not on the evidence of millions of years of evolutionary survival, but on mere faith. In addition, it is a faith in a process that has arguably increased risk in its small time of existence, or at least has the potential to do so. Do we place our trust in the possibility of achieving some safe haven based on some heretofore unrealized technological miracle, or in the miracle of the wider universe that has evolved before us? If it is in the latter, then faith should be placed on achieving natural order, not mere technological progress.

To argue that progress must always entail some possibility of disaster leads to the *paradox of progress*. Some ideal place, our *utopia*, can only be achieved under the threat of possible annihilation. This idea presents a very hopeless view of progress. Progress toward what, we might ask? The answer is eventual extinction. Not a particularly appealing tradeoff.

Of course, no one wants to go back to primitive times. The thought of life 100 years ago brings to mind hardships that most of us, from our modern vantage point, simply would not want to endure. Yet there is a choice to be made here, in terms of the true value of life. When it comes to choosing between the relatively comfortable life many of us lead now and survival, the question of value arises, in a big way. We will discuss the notion of valuing our survival, within the concept of a natural balance of life, later on. For now, we would suggest that there may be circumstances in our imperfectly known future that may make some degree of primitivism, or at least a return to more basic values, the more attractive option. Of course, we all hope we never have to really go back to that level. Neither do we want to succumb to extinction, however.

The assessment of danger in this way should be part of every decision process with respect to safe progress. If some action brings about the genuine potential for catastrophic risk, we need to avoid it, at least until we can figure out some way to make it safe (i.e., conform to natural risk levels). Say someone develops a shampoo that does a superb job at providing clean hair, at a fraction of the price of current products. The only problem is it turns your hair purple. The product would not be considered saleable under these conditions, and it is back to the design and testing phase for its originator. The same should occur for any activity judged unsafe. The activity, in this regard, has simply not yet been perfected, and the general public should not be exposed until it is.

3.5 Recognizing the uncertainties

As is the case with the probabilities of rare, high impact events, the threshold between "risky" and "not risky" exposures is fuzzy. We simply do not have sufficient knowledge of this complex process we call risk to be able to define the dividing line precisely. How could we reasonably identify a one in a million chance of disaster as not risky, and yet a one in nine hundred and ninety-nine thousand (a difference of one hundredth of a thousand) as not? Realistically, only an imprecise division can be identified. This division is informed by the existence of various natural risk levels consistent with human and ecological evolution through time. Some very low probability events will be classified as not risky, with confidence. On the other hand, we might identify certain risk levels as unequivocally risky, in relation to the types of risk we find in a more natural setting. In between, there are likelihoods that can only be identified as fitting the ideas of risky and not risky to various degrees.

In Figure 3.1 we show a simple representation of the *danger zone*, in terms of the probabilities and impact of an event. Probabilities range from certain ("1") to some very small number. Tiny probabilities, though they do not exclude physical possibility, are small enough to be considered practically impossible. In turn, events with likelihoods greater than these are considered possible. Potential outcomes range from small to catastrophic. The danger zone as represented in this probability/loss

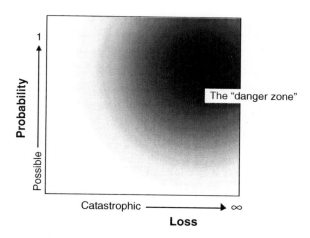

Figure 3.1 The "danger zone"

space is defined by the intersection of the fuzzy ideas of possibility and catastrophe. As a result, the region itself can only be identified in a fuzzy fashion. Some probability/loss combinations are clearly dangerous, while others are as clearly not. In between lies a fuzzy range on uncertainty where we might declare that an exposure is somewhat dangerous, or possibly dangerous, and act accordingly.

Risk acceptance studies frequently focus on precise risk levels, thereby engendering unending and ultimately unnecessary debate on where the exact risk thresholds should lie. Rather than pursuing the futile task of trying to identify some exact level of likelihood as acceptable or not, we should rather be refining our inherently fuzzy notion of risk, making it, if not more precise, at least more accurate as a representation of what we do and do not know about high-stakes risks and how they could harm us.

As in the case of probability assessment, intervals and related fuzzy interpretations of some property can give us useful information, even though it is imperfect. Our goal then is not to obscure these imperfections or otherwise assume them away. We need to work to make the uncertainty inherent in such assessments useful to us.

3.6   Avoiding danger in an uncertain world

The danger zone is a region of probability/impact combinations bounded by losses that are sufficiently high to be called catastrophic, and at the same time of sufficient likelihood so as to exceed natural levels. To apply the idea of precautionary avoidance in an uncertain world, we match the imperfectly known probabilities and impacts of an exposure to our fuzzy definition of danger. Those that provide a sufficient fit with the concept of danger are avoided. For example, earthquakes in Florida are an exceedingly rare phenomenon. Given the seismic history, and inferences from the geology of the region, the likelihood of a devastating earthquake in Florida simply does not extend into the risky region in any realistic sense. On the other hand, certain chemical substances, such as benzene or asbestos, show demonstrated probabilities of harm that are clearly high. This, in turn, places them firmly in the dangerous region.

The likelihood of other exposures may be imperfectly known. Scientists are unable to identify an exact probability for adverse effects of genetically modified crops, for instance. We may suspect that a tremendous negative potential exists, and that there is not sufficient theoretical or practical evidence to exclude the possibility of disaster (unlike the case of earthquakes in Florida). Precaution demands that we treat such unknown, yet potentially disastrous, exposures *as if* they were dangerous, and act accordingly. A similar case could be built, for example, around the uncertainty surrounding extreme effects of human-produced global warming.

The process is shown in Figure 3.2. Exposure (a), representing perhaps our assessment of the effects on humans and the environment of known carcinogens such as benzene, is unequivocally risky, falling fully within the danger zone. On the other hand, exposure (b), representing, say, drinking pure water, can be classified as non-risky with equal confidence. In between we have those very imperfectly known events, such as global warming or genetically modified crops, which due to their uncertainty may make them *possibly* risky (e.g., exposure (c), whose uncertainty band extends into the danger zone). A proper *uncertainty modified* version of precaution would suggest that these too be avoided, at least until we can more adequately determine where their likelihoods and impacts lie. Just how uncertain an event should be to qualify as dangerous (i.e., the degree

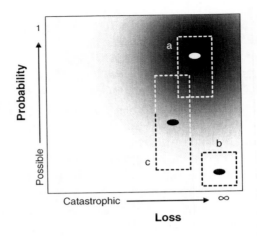

Figure 3.2   Is exposure "c" risky?

of overlap between imperfectly known probabilities and the danger zone) is a matter of investigation and determination based on stakeholders interests, and clearly an area for further study.

We can also see from this analysis why fully identifying the uncertainties involved in high-stakes risk assessment is so important. If we had, for example, used only the best guess estimate to identify the riskiness of exposure (c), we might have reasonably deemed it not risky, even under the fuzzy definition of risk threshold. Self-interested manipulation of risk studies is therefore a distinct possibility when uncertainty is ignored, or disguised. The uncertainty associated with risk decisions matters. It could be the difference between life and death. Uncertainty, over and above the uncertainty associated with randomness, needs to be taken into consideration when making properly precautionary decisions about high-stakes risk. This is an example of how both uncertainty due to knowledge imperfections and the catastrophe problem ("in the long run, there may be no long run") intertwine to make high-stakes decisions especially difficult.

In assessing danger, we have in mind a rough but useful definition of risk that fits our natural intuition of background, or natural, risk level. In managing the risks of life, we assess, however imperfectly, the likelihood of bad outcomes. This matching process therefore becomes less of a matter of measurement of risk and more about its *recognition*. High-stakes risk management is about recognizing patterns in the very uncertain information we have. We assess both what we do know and what we don't know about the catastrophic potentials of some exposures, and based on that potentials inherent in that (naturally) fuzzy estimate, we see if that exposure "fits" our rough notion of risk.

This *pattern recognition* approach to risk suggests a very natural fit of the process of assuring survival from risky exposures. We identify, often very imperfectly, our goals, and then establish suitable means, themselves fuzzy, for achieving these goals. While outcomes will be imperfect, we trust them to be suitably definite so as to achieve the goals of life using as fully as possible the natural gift of perception and reasoning we were born with.

3.7   How uncertainty complicates decisions about the *accumulation* of risk

So far, we have only looked at potential high-stakes risk exposures individually, assessing single case likelihoods of danger. In the real world, multiple risk exposures can accumulate, increasing the potential for danger. Recognizing the great uncertainty inherent in identifying models of high-stakes risk, any accumulation of risk will itself be fuzzy. This uncertainty arises from two sources. First of all, we cannot precisely measure the probability of disaster arising from the accumulation of sources of risk. The world, as we have argued above, is simply too uncertain. Again, the uncertainty reflected here is based on knowledge imperfection, not randomness. When our knowledge of probabilities is imperfect, the best we can do is specify rough intervals of uncertainty, possibly graded by credibility (i.e., fuzziness) of the estimates. In assessing the impact of this growth, we need a proper definition of what is risky. Once again, knowledge imperfection enters. We can only specify risk thresholds imperfectly.

The resulting fuzzy representation of accumulation may look something like Figure 3.3. As risks accumulate, the possibility of disaster increases. Under a model with so many uncertainties, the best we can do is identify roughly three categories of risk as growing through accumulation: Impossibility, possibility, and certainty. The only way to assure survival then is to prevent the accumulation of risk, that is, *treat all risks on a precautionary basis.*

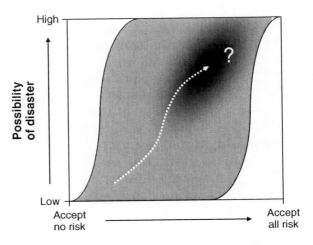

Figure 3.3 A "fuzzy" representation of risk accumulation

Also shown in the figure is some hypothetical fuzzy path for the growth of risk ("progress"). The unknown path reflects the fact that precise knowledge of both the probabilities and the impacts of risk growth is a fiction. No pathway can be reasonably identified with confidence. The shaded area in fact represents a bundle of possible pathways, some very seriously negative. By extending formal models of risk accumulation to include the inherent uncertainties, we paint a far more serious picture of risk accumulation. What we don't know *can* hurt us.

Recognizing the extremely fuzzy nature of risk accumulation has significant impacts on the way we manage risk. How might the fuzzy interpretation of risk influence policy, especially risk management? For one thing, it suggests that we may enter an unknown and potentially quite dangerous region very quickly. On the other hand, the inherent uncertainty means that we can't know that with any degree of reliability. We may be safer than we think. A suitably precautionary stance, however, demands that we pay attention to the negative possibilities. As a result, we can infer that the fuzzy potential suggests that we avoid risk accumulation, as strictly as possible. That means, for example, adhering to tight (albeit somewhat fuzzy) risk acceptance criteria based on very low, natural risk levels for individual exposures.

The fuzzy interpretation also means that should we somehow find ourselves at the higher end of the possibility scale, the way back to safety may not be obvious. Actions in an attempt to reduce risk are not guaranteed to have the effect of reducing risk. The fuzzy frontier entails some quite possibly discontinuous, even chaotic, pathways. Responses to the threat of global warming today are a case in point. Considerable uncertainty surrounds the path back toward safe levels of human-produced carbon accumulation in the atmosphere. Some scientists have indeed raised the question of whether we may have already gone too far to reduce the potentially catastrophic long-term effects by simply reducing future emissions. The uncertainty that surrounds this issue is typified by the foggy gray area of fuzziness in our model.

Last but not least, a risk management response based on prioritization of risk does not make sense under the fuzzy model. Should we find ourselves at some high-possibility point, we once again cannot be sure where the adjustment of single risks will get us. The idea of "bigger" risk becomes clouded. The suggestion again, in terms of the all-or-nothing character of high-stakes risk under very uncertain conditions, is that assurance can only come from the elimination of all risks (or at least a reduction to below some natural risk level). These risk management factors are summarized in Figure 3.4.

The question becomes, how can we achieve and maintain the avoidance of risk? From the standpoint of maintenance, we have suggested that it requires a commitment to a subsistence level of risk consistent with natural background levels that have sustained life on this planet for millions of years. Our ingenuity is then channeled into determining how we get past this subsistence level and achieve progress, without sliding down

---

1. Fuzzy accumulation suggests the importance of a genuinely precautionary approach: What we don't know *can* hurt us.
2. Should we find ourselves in a position of concern about risk growth, fuzziness suggests that reducing risk may not be as simple as retracing our steps (i.e., "backtracking").
3. Under fuzziness, the idea of "prioritizing" risks doesn't make sense. How do we know which risk is worse? After all, all it takes is one.

Figure 3.4 Risk management implications of fuzzy accumulation of risk

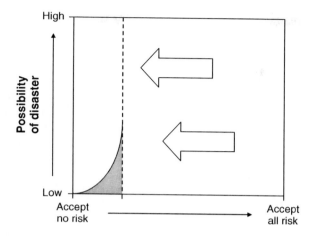

Figure 3.5 Precautionary "hold-back" of risk

that fuzzy slope toward disaster. The more troubling issue is reducing risks that *already* exist. Based on the risk management factors associated with fuzzy accumulation, there remains the possibility that recognition of this accumulation may in fact come too late.

Risk avoidance, then, provides for a precautionary "hold-back" (or, applied later in time, a "push-back") of risk, as shown in Figure 3.5. By implementing properly precautionary strategies, we can reduce *both* the threat to existence and the uncertainty surrounding it. What hope we have for reducing worry about our existence, the true aim of risk management, comes from our ability to achieve and maintain this level of security.

Further reading

The idea of natural risk based on the survival of the earth itself includes the recent work of physicist Max Tegmark and philosopher Nick Bostrom, "How Unlikely is a Doomsday Catastrophe?", in *Nature*, December 7, 2005. The authors conclude life on our planet is highly unlikely to be annihilated by an exogenous catastrophe, for example, a cosmic ray collision, during the next 10^9 (10 billion) years.

Various risk acceptance criteria, including the natural approach, are reviewed in a book by Barcuh Fischoff and colleagues entitled *Acceptable Risk: A Critical Guide* (Cambridge University Press, 1984). Sir Martin Rees chronicles a variety of modern risks, distinguishing them from "baseline natural risks", in *Our Final Hour: A Scientist's Warning* (Basic Books, 2003). Despite the ominous title, Rees presents a level-headed discussion of the facts behind the growth of existential risks. For more on the various notions of risk acceptability in a societal framework, see *Understanding and Responding to Societal Concerns*, by David Ball and Sonja Boehmer-Christiansen (HSE Books, 2002).

On the notions of "impossibility", including its relation to knowledge, possibility, and complexity, see John D. Barrow's *Impossibility: Limits of Science and the Science of Limits* (Vintage, 2004). On the distinction between the various underlying theories of probability related to the notion of *physical* possibility, including great discussions of both the frequency and propensity interpretations, see D. Gillies, *Philosophical Theories of Probability* (Routledge, 2000).

4
Where Are We Now?

The fuzzy nature of high-stakes risk suggests that it may be difficult to tell just how risky the world has become, at least before it is too late. Recognizing that, up to this point in our history at least, the dominant response has been the sort of fatalism based on acquiescence, we may not be in a very good place with respect to risk. Fanciful application of statistical techniques to a domain in which they have no relevance enforces this somewhat negative view. A reasonable assessment of the facts suggests that we may be living in a world where "un-natural" acts have tipped the scale toward disaster. In fact, there may be manifestations of this increased danger occurring today.

In light of these facts, it may also be instructive to take a look at how we might have gotten to this place. Even though the ultimate risks may still be imperfectly known, we do know that a long history of warnings has existed, most promulgated by whom we might identify as *radical rethinkers* of our path toward progress. After all, cogent warnings can only be ignored for so long. Last but not least, we take a look at the idea that the world we live in is indeed the *best possible world*. This approach suggests that voluntary acceptance by rational humans is the best indicator of "natural" risk levels. The best possible world approach and voluntary acceptance of risk often rely on a sort of optimism about the future. That is, what dangers that lurk can be overcome by future advancements in science and technology. Our teleological view, based on natural order, suggests a more realistic approach. Depending on the very thinking that got us into an unsavory position with respect to existential risk to get us out is not optimistic, it's foolish.

Part of the realistic approach to high-stakes risk is realizing that while these indicators of increased risk are not certain, the *uncertainty* they entail can itself have equally deleterious effects. We do not go so far here as to prognosticate that if we don't do something now, disaster *will* occur. On the other hand, uncertainty *does* matter to how we live our lives. And by all indications, the uncertainty surrounding survival has never been greater.

4.1   Current manifestations of a more dangerous world

Just what are the high-stakes risks we face today, that is, those that might fall into society's *danger zone*? An increasing number of global risk assessments are being promulgated, many through somewhat dense ideological filters. Most of these filters are applied with selfish interests in mind. The large chemical company is concerned about global market demand risks, while ignoring (or at least downplaying) the risk of production-related pollution. This lopsided endeavor is codified in the rise of enterprise-wide risk management efforts of the modern business entity. While ostensibly holistic, such efforts usually result in a blind eye toward the propagation of external risks. As a result, many global risk assessments tend to obscure the inconvenient.

- Political/social unrest
- Pollution/technological excess
- Economic crisis/collapse
- Income/class inequality
- Lifestyle/health challenges
- Population pressure
- Energy resources/markets

Figure 4.1 Global risks: the *Unlucky 7*

Offered here is, if not a more accurate view of the risks we face, at least a more realistic one. We reduce the assessment to what we might call the *Unlucky 7* risk types, as shown in Figure 4.1. The probability and loss characteristics of these risks cannot be known for certain. The only thing we know with a strong sense of confidence is that these risks present significant increases in risk above natural levels. To the extent that such a risk identification exercise presents merely a prelude to some form of risk management based on prioritization, they are worthless. The true value of such assessments lies in making us aware of the enormity of our task. Genuine comfort can only come when the associated risk levels are reduced below natural levels.

While our view of these risks is necessarily fuzzy, we might wonder if there are at least some indications that would suggest how real they are. Might there be in the very imperfect picture of these loss potentials some vague indications of what we face, in terms of high-stake risks and their effects? We would suggest that there do indeed exist signals in our world today that influence our imminent health, happiness and survival. Many of these signs are a product of what we might call manifestations of gradual or *creeping* risk. Among the highest ranked hazards related to individual fatalities today are heart disease, cancer, workplace injuries (especially in high hazard employments), cerebro-vascular disease, and automobile accidents. Can these risks be considered genuinely natural? We would say not. One hundred years ago, the list was topped by diseases such as pneumonia, tuberculosis, and enteritis. They were a reflection of the times in which our modern society was developing.

Many have been eradicated, based on advancements in applying natural hygiene to a modern, industrialized world, along with mechanisms to distribute these health improvements among a rapidly growing population. So, why replace such relatively simple diseases with those so much more complex to treat? In many cases, the new killers are related to environmental factors, most of which we might reasonably associate with progress as it is narrowly defined, for example, in terms of economic growth.

4.2   Down the path to disaster

If we are genuinely in such a bad place, or at least suspect we might be, how did we get here? Some suggest that certain "surprises" along the path to progress are unavoidable. The idea is supported by the belief that in many cases, both in terms of natural and human-made risks, there exists an unfathomable ignorance. Many argue that such "temporary" ignorance is pervasive, and such risks are bound to arise upon us suddenly and unexpectedly. How can we guard against what we don't know? The best response then is to deal with these risks as they arise, with the hope that we might identify some adequate scientific or technological solutions before it is too late.

The problem with this conception is that we are not so collectively ignorant of risk as some people suggest. That global climate change, for example, has come upon us suddenly is ridiculous. Warnings about the adverse possibility of industrial carbon buildup have been around since at least the early 1960s. That we needed the type of conclusive proof that scientific investigations are currently developing (e.g., measurements of polar ice melts) is also preposterous, and downright dangerous. By waiting until science can prove a disaster potential exists beyond a shadow of a doubt we may find that it is too late to do something about it. As we have pointed out, a great deal of uncertainty about the high-stakes risk we face arises from deep, and perhaps irreducible, knowledge imperfections. However, to say that these knowledge imperfections are pervasive, that we ultimately face the *unknown-unknown*, leaves us unable to take any action. Action therefore becomes completely subjective.

Rather than facing a pervasive ignorance (the genuinely *unknowable*), it is likely that the most challenging high-stakes problem involves the recognition of risk on an imperfect yet useful basis. We may know, or at least suspect, certain deficiencies in our knowledge exist. When we do so, we take this type of uncertainty into consideration in our decision-making. This is exactly what precautionary risk management rules demand: If in doubt, we proceed with extra caution. Precaution is therefore an approach not only to managing risk but also to *managing uncertainties about risk*.

In many cases, claims of "unknown" risks for some activity are merely a cover for self-interested promotion of that activity, and ultimately an excuse for ignoring the warning signs. Risk grows through inattention, either intentional or unintentional, to its uncertain nature. We can defend against ignorance, yet it is harder to defend against being intentionally misled, especially by a crafty opponent. In this regard the idea of "no progress without risk" amounts to a misrepresentation, a fraudulent inducement toward progress without properly under-standing the costs. The whole process is akin to the classic *bait and switch* sales scam. A store advertises a product at some very attractive price. You drive to the store, incurring some degree of sunk cost in the process, and upon your arrival are told that the advertised prod-uct is no longer available, Instead, you may purchase a roughly equivalent product, at a much higher cost. By not buying, your sunk costs (the drive to the store) are for nothing. Any way you look, you are, in effect, stuck with more expense than you bargained for. In accepting progress against risk, we build sunk costs that catch us in a dilemma once the true "price" of progress becomes known.

When in doubt, especially with regard to those events that may cause extinction, it makes sense to take pre-cautions. The only other logical choice is to not care. We can't know where we are, so we can't do anything about it, so... why worry? Again, we are back to a dis-tinctly fatalistic position which in and of itself cannot be gainsaid. It is what it is. In the area between lies the potential for cajoling, fooling, misguiding, and even coercing actions that we deem in our own self-interest, disregarding the wider interests of others (including those of the natural world itself). The unknown must not be confused with the disguised. Our challenge is properly distinguishing between the two.

On the face of it, it would seem as though some sort of fatalism is the dominant philosophy with respect to risk today. When we do face high-stakes risks on a for-mal basis, it is often on the basis of some ill-conceived cost-benefit basis. As we have argued above, most formal risk assessment using modern decision theory and the theory of expected utility maximization is just a form of disguised fatalism. Fatalism, in the sense of natural order, is not good or bad. It does not mean acceptance of inevitable doom. Mere acquiescence, however, is a sign of giving up. A deeper look at the risk we face suggests that we need to carefully distinguish between a genuinely held fatalism based on our ability to live life in harmony with natural risks and a forced acquiescence based on tricks and cajolery that ultimately serve only to promote special interests.

4.3   The rise of complex socio-technological interactions

Today's landscape of existential risk is further complicated by the rise of what we might call socio-technological interactions among risks. These interactions involve the melding of technological risks with social ones. Technological risks include those associated with the scientific and technical aspects of survival, and include the risks of pollution from human-made substances, and misuse of technological developments. Social risks include increased geopolitical strife and inequality.

One source of interaction is due to the fact that technological exposures to risk, and the uncertainty they create, are not uniformly distributed among the world's population. The economically poorer, the disadvantaged in terms of social and economic status, arguably bear the greater exposures to risks. Risks to our survival are made more uncertain when our proximity to potential sources and our general ability to protect ourselves from possible risks decreases. We could argue as well that the natural elements of the earth, such as animal and plant life, might be the most disadvantaged of all, as having the least ability to defend against artificially created risk potentials.

The complex, and disturbing, nature of these socio-technological interactions is perhaps most plain with respect to the threat of nuclear conflict, either in the context of explicitly declared war or carried out via various terrorist tactics included in undeclared, guerilla warfare. Nuclear weapons have brought damage of truly monumental proportions into the realm of possibility. One hundred years ago, the cannonball was the "weapon of mass destruction". To lay this potential at the feet of progress is perhaps going too far, yet the correlation is inescapable. Nowhere is the adage that with great power comes great responsibility so true. The use of nuclear weapons has become its own dilemma of sorts, as to give up nuclear weapons unilaterally is viewed by the major powers of the world today as a simply untenable position, in light of assuring their own survival.

The answer lies in a rethinking of social relationships, not just technological ones. The interaction of the two, however, is clear. When faced with one existential risk, does it make sense to incur another to counterbalance this risk? It may not make perfect logical sense, yet it may be the only choice under extreme social duress. Once again, the answer is not technological – but rather must be constructed socially and politically, in consideration of its technological aspects.

From the social and political perspective, we need to ask ourselves, to what extent have our economic and social institutions brought us to where we are now? Once we identify those defects, we need to fix them. That is, as we shall see, where some idea of planning and control comes in. Such planning then becomes part of maintaining a natural order, and is not to be seen as manipulative in any sense. Just as we consider the need to control basic bodily functions like breathing and body temperature as non-manipulative, so must be the idea of social planning for a natural order.

4.4 Confusing forced acceptance with naturalness

To cut through the complex issues of uncertainties and interactions, we might view the reactions of the decision-makers themselves. We have observed that the dominant approach to high-stakes risk today may be some sort of fatalism, or acceptance, of risk. Might this acceptance by rational decision-makers be a sign that what is acceptable should be viewed as "natural"? Related to a purely utilitarian view of moral conduct is the belief that how we actually act with respect to risk reflects the *best* way to act. After all, why would we act against our own best interests? We would suggest that in many cases the decision is purely one of acquiescence, or forced acceptance. We cannot argue the choice is made freely, when there simply is no other choice. To use such *forced* choices to set risk criteria is improper. In many cases, what we consider a rationally fatalistic response may simply be one of resignation.

The crucial presumption under the utilitarian view is that all risk acceptance is voluntary. Willing acceptance may, however, simply be a sign that we have become *desensitized* to risk. We accept risk because we believe, or are made to believe, we have no choice. Current risk levels, no matter how high they are, are legitimized by the fact that they exist. The question becomes, how much longer will we continue to exist under such conditions?

Based on the belief that we have no choice, we can make the 40,000 deaths a year from automobiles in the United States, and over 2 million worldwide, seem like a natural risk. They are after all part of the way of modern life. Yet, we would not argue for a risk threshold based on the 30,000 suicides that occur in the United States each year, would we? Or on the basis of observed homicides?

Certain voluntary behaviors may in fact be pathological. Pathologies should not serve as a criterion for rational risk acceptance.

A wide literature has developed around the notion that when intuition disagrees with the normative standards of statistical expected value decision it is intuition which is faulty. This psychological approach to risk suggests that humans make systematic errors resulting in a biased approach to risk acceptance and denial. The base of this approach, however, is a misguided belief in the axiomatic correctness of expected value decision as the truly normative approach to risk. Again, while these observations may be applicable to the statistical world (people probably aren't really good intuitive statisticians) it has little or no relevance to the high-stakes domain. The idea that aversion to catastrophe is "all in our heads" is a fiction, though convenient to those that may seek to promote specialized agendas.

There is a tendency to consider progress itself as a purely natural phenomenon. As a result, we confuse what "is" with what "ought" to be. The problem for such optimists, which no lesser a mind than the great philosopher of optimism Leibniz himself struggled with, is reconciling the imperfections of the world. This tendency to rationalize imperfections – to believe that despite its imperfections, we live in the *best possible world* – continues to this day. It is essential to the thought of those who would downplay the existence of existential risks. It also underlies incremental approaches to risk reductions which suggest that accepting existential risk is all part of our idea of progress. Unfortunately, such an approach relies too much on the good intentions of our fellow humans. And as such, like acquiescence in general, it makes our thoughts subject to manipulation. The success in this manipulation may lie in what we want to believe, as opposed to what we should.

Does a belief in nature simply reverse the fallacy? A commitment to natural risk levels does not require assuming all of nature is benign. Nor will adhering to natural risk levels eliminate all tragic choices – the mother bear will still sacrifice herself to protect her cubs from a natural predator. However, understanding how to live within the boundaries of nature, as we have more widely construed it, is part of human wisdom – itself a by-product of human nature. Recognizing that this wider nature has existed long before humans, and will undoubtedly continue long after, it is more reasonable that we learn to live within its boundaries, rather than forcing it to conform to ours.

4.5   What's next?

Most calls for action in the face of risk usually end with rather dire predictions, of the sort "If we don't take proper action, we will surely perish." The idea is presumably to shock the general public out of mere acquiescence, and into critical thinking about the risks we face. The problem with such unqualified statements of impending doom is that they cannot logically provide a precise timetable. The temptation then is to make up one that is suitably disturbing to provoke action. The problem with using such predictions of doom to incite action is that without some reasonably immediate framework, they will have no effect on the current generation of decision-makers. This means that predictions aimed at inciting such action envision a horizon of 20 or 30 years, optimally placed at roughly half a modern lifetime. Given the history of modern warnings, beginning in most potency, say in the early to mid-1960s, some 30 or 40 years have past since these original doom predictions, and we have yet survived. The predictions are falsified and, as a result, their initial shock effect is considerably diluted.

Given the uncertainties, prognostications about the exact date of pending disaster are worthless. It is these uncertainties, however, which provide the greatest impetus for critical action. Arguably, it is this uncertainty which has increased over the last 30 or 40 years of modern development. As a result, it is this uncertainty that we should be most concerned about, not whether doom will occur or not occur tomorrow, or the next day. It is *not knowing* that should produce action, not the prognostication that in 20 or 30 years we all won't be here. Is our next draw from the urn of futures random, or has it been influenced in some unknown way? Is the ball marked "disaster" immediately under our finger tips, ready to be pulled?

So, "what's next" is not doom *for sure*...but it may be. As a result of the mounting uncertainties, we just don't know. So while the last 30 or 40 years have not provided irrefutable evidence that the end is near, they have provided concrete evidence that *we may not have done enough to avoid such possibilities*. As the intuitive notion of precaution suggests, however, even though we don't know the end may be near in the foreseeable future, we might want to act like it is – just in case. Under this form of reasoning, the fact that we are still here 30 or 40 years after the initial wave of warnings about risk might mean that we are just lucky. This short span of survival is certainly not enough to surmount the inherent uncertainties involved. In this sense, the warnings of years past are still completely valid – even thought they haven't come true, yet. And still a comprehensive precautionary approach remains virtually non-existent in modern social and economic policy.

Critics of a precautionary approach suggest that the emphasis on the potential for risk is overblown, creating an undue alarmism. They often point to voluntary acceptance of risk, clinging to a best possible world approach. Ignored is the fact that such acceptance is often forced, and may in fact provide no choice. Some go as far as to argue that these fears may be a sign that we are *too* safe. The safety of our times means we have nothing better to do than worry about maintaining it. Once again, the extreme uncertainties we face mitigate against the idea that we can afford to comfort ourselves by believing that threats to our survival are all a figment of a wayward imagination.

One thing for certain is that people's rational understanding of where we are now with respect to existential risk cannot be suppressed for long. We can fool some of the people some of the time, but not all the people, all the time. Flimsy arguments for the best possible world based on perceived voluntary acceptance of possible disaster, pseudo-scientific risk assessments, and a reliance on optimism in the face of allegedly unknown risks are bound to fall apart as uncertainty about the safety of our world builds. The results will not be reflected in made up proxies for our state of collective well-being, but in the actions of those affected.

Further reading

For a comprehensive review of the high-stakes risks we face today, one of the best sources of unbiased information remains the World Watch Institute's annual *Vital Signs* report. The Institute annually convenes a panel of experts to assess trends in categories including food, agricultural resources, energy and climate, global economy, resource economics, the environment, conflict and peace, communications and transportation, population and society, and health and disease.

Recognition of the potential adverse side effects of the uncertainties associated with technical progress has a long history. Precautionary responses to uncertainty go at least as far back as George Perkins Marsh in the mid-1800s. Marsh's *Man and Nature* (Charles Scribner, 1865) marked the beginning of a movement toward conservation of our natural environment in the face of the onslaught of technological (and social) progress, which was reflected in the work of natural conservationists into the twentieth century. We could reasonably argue, however, that the modern awakening of risk issues accompanying the new era of industrial and social progress began with Barry Commoner's *Science and Survival* (Viking Press), published in 1966. While preceded by select warnings on specific technological and scientific risks in the tradition of the new radical rethinking of risk and progress (including Commoner's own warnings on the perils of atmospheric testing of atomic weapons and Rachel Carson's notable examination of the negative effects of the pesticide DDT in *Silent Spring* [Houghton Mifflin, 1962]), *Science and Survival* brought the issue to the public in full form. The tone and direction of that book, including its call for what was effectively a precautionary approach to high-stakes risk under uncertainty, shapes the debate to this day.

As we have suggested, a great deal of the debate about high-stakes risk may be formed in an atmosphere of less than complete honesty by those that would promote short-sighted self-interests over long-term survival. For a discussion of the *bait-and-switch*, and other less than honest practices, see *The Complete Idiot's Guide to Frauds, Scams, and Cons* (Alpha Publishing, 2002), by David Swierczynski.

For a discussion of the disparate exposure of the world's social and economic classes to high-stakes risks, and its sociopolitical effects, see Tom Athanansiou's *Divided Planet: The Ecology of the Rich and the Poor* (University of Georgia Press, 1998). Further issues of equality and justice in environmental health and risk-taking are explored in Kristen Shrader-Frechett's *Environmental Justice: Creating Equality, Reclaiming Democracy* (Oxford University Press, 2005).

The impact of uncertainty on citizen concerns and activism regarding high-stakes environmental risks is discussed in *Uncertain Hazards: Environmental Activists and Scientific Proof* (Cornell University Press, 2000), by Sylvia Noble Tesh. See also Kristen Shrader-Frechette's *Burying Uncertainty: Risk and the Case Against Geological Disposal of Radioactive Wastes* (University of California Press, 1994). There is a long experimental and observational history that decision-makers respond with considerable anxiety to even the more mundane decisions in life when probabilities are imperfectly known. See, for example, the review by Colin Camerer and Martin Weber, "Recent Developments in Modeling Preferences: Uncertainty and Ambiguity", *Journal of Risk and Uncertainty*, October, 1992. Unfortunately, the impact of uncertainty on political and social unrest remains underappreciated, and understudied.

5
Planning for a Safer Future

Given the complexities of our existence, we cannot effectively achieve natural risk levels without some sort of deliberate forethought, or *planning*. That means setting goals, and identifying safe alternatives that can help us achieve these goals. Reliance on simple statistical approaches that attempt to adjust progress only when problems become apparent just doesn't work for risks where the cost of mistakes can be enormous. This means that planning for safe progress needs to take into consideration both the uncertain nature of the risks we face and the fact that we don't get a second chance to make the right decisions. This tricky balance challenges our ingenuity to the fullest. We need to identify and implement a process that *fails safe* with regard to existential risk. If progress cannot be made safely, we forestall further action until we figure out how it can.

We develop here a perspective on planning and related control techniques for the management of high-stakes risk based on the idea of working backward from the ideal of naturally risk-free living. In the process, we identify alternative courses of action to achieve this ideal. This approach assures a properly precautionary attitude, without the side effects of entrenched risks. In the planning process, teleology, or sense of purpose, combines with ideas for action to provide a more complete model for risk management of high-stakes outcomes. In planning for a safer future, we plan for a world in which survivability *matters*.

5.1 Avoiding risk dilemmas

We have shown that when applying a suitable natural threshold to high-stakes risk, *everything is not risky*. Many things still are, however. The problem with applying precaution to these residual risks is that the minimax approach commits us to spend *up to* the potential cost of the largest possible loss in order to prevent it. More colloquially, precaution can be *expensive*. The cost of prevention may itself present us with a difficult choice. Taking precautionary actions may result in counter-risks that leave us "doomed if we do, doomed if we don't". We refer to these challenges to effective precautionary behavior as *risk dilemmas*.

The modern concern over climate change and global warming is an example of such a risk dilemma. If we continue along the current path of industrial progress fueled, literally, by hydrocarbon sources, we may eventually incur a global climate catastrophe. Eliminating or even substantially reducing industrial progress in an attempt to curb warming could itself have serious, possibly catastrophic, side effects. Sudden economic collapse could entail physical extinction.

The *American Heritage Dictionary* defines a dilemma as "a choice between equally balanced alternatives, most often unattractive ones". In the case of risk dilemmas, the choice is between two potentially fatal results. To complicate things further, one or more of these choices may depend on unknown chances. This uncertain character makes weighing one option against another difficult, if not impossible. Given the final nature of each, do such incremental differences even matter? Like the notion of precaution itself, the way to avoid dilemmas is very simple, in theory at least: We avoid risk dilemmas by not getting into them in the first place. And like precaution, this anticipatory approach faces great practical challenges. As we will argue in what follows, none are insurmountable. The solutions may, however, require substantial personal and systematic change.

5.2 The problem with short-run risk control techniques

Short-run statistical risk planning relies on a mode of control that depends on periodic feedback on the possible negative side effects of progress. This type of planning is embodied in the *identify–assess–treat (I-A-T) model* of risk management (Figure 5.1). We identify potential sources of risk, assess options based on that analysis, and treat the problem accordingly. Given the statistical nature of the endeavor, we can adjust our course of

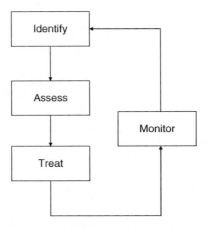

Figure 5.1 The *identify–assess–treat (I-A-T) model* of risk management

action based on observing relatively immediate outcomes. For this reason, feedback control is often used to assess the quality of production processes, for example. We set quality goals, say in terms of tolerance measurements of some manufactured component – maybe a screw or a bolt. As production goes on, it is subject to various random forces that can degrade quality, like, for example, machine wear or misalignment. In statistical quality control, a sample of output is periodically extracted, measured against goal, and adjustments are made to the process as needed. These adjustments may entail replacement of production equipment, or its readjustment. Such planning efforts need not rely on a specific model of the exposure, and are relatively quick to react to changes. The drawback is that the effects of risk have to manifest themselves within a relatively narrow window of observation. The longer it takes to recognize the path of risk, the more difficult to make a subsequent correction. With regard to high-stakes risk, the statistical approach runs into the "catastrophe problem".

Analysis based on statistical feedback can easily miss larger, long-term trends, such as those that characterize catastrophic loss potentials. In this case, we can find that catastrophic risks become entrenched before our simple feedback system has time to respond. The result of applying treatment at this late stage is incurring great cost, as we attempt to undo what has already been done. We find ourselves faced with a risk dilemma. As a result, simple feedback control systems, and the progressive planning they entail, are not appropriate for tackling the fundamental catastrophe problem.

5.3 The importance of *preaction*

Looking at the simple, static decision matrix for high-stakes losses (like Figure 2.3, above), it seems as though the precautionary choice is obvious from the outset. Yet factors may serve to obscure the potential rise of risk dilemmas as time goes on. We may start with a risk situation in which our decision matrix may be populated with some fairly innocuous risks. Our decision might be to accept these risks on a statistical basis. Yet, over time, risks can grow. And so will the costs of mitigating or eliminating them. At some later time, the decision matrix may entail the risk dilemma. Avoiding the risk at that time can cost as much as resigning ourselves to it.

It is obvious from the dynamic nature of risk that the key to making precautionary actions acceptable hinges on the *timing* of our actions. We need to take precaution *before* it becomes "too late". The approach is one of *preaction* rather than simple reaction. We plan for safe progress, thereby avoiding future dilemmas of the "doomed if you do, doomed if you don't" variety. In this way, what may seem to be costs under one world view are really no more than actions necessary to facilitate continued existence.

By acting in a suitably advanced fashion, we reconcile survival with leading the high life, supported in turn by a *realistic* optimism. As we have noted, fatalism is the very condition of life. This fatalism pushes us toward some goal, some deeper purpose. Our destiny is to go along with this flow. This means coordinating our actions, and responsibilities, to match this deeper purpose. When do the "do nothing" and the survival aspects of our risk decision matrix coincide? Fatalism and precaution are one when we take a natural path to risk-free existence. We achieve our goal of survival within the natural system, by doing what comes naturally. We live the proper life with respect to our responsibilities, and this naturalness amounts to doing nothing, or at least nothing extraordinary.

By proper forethought and the seeking out of safe alternative pathways to progress, we can achieve a truly better life, including one in which we live in relative *freedom from risk*. The trick, of course, is being able to assess such course of action from the beginning, and making sure we steer the proper course. This, in turn, requires more scientific endeavor than simply waiting for things happen. To be effective, however, science must focus on prevention of risk as well as seeking other goals we might consider compatible with a better life. The main point here is that safe progress requires commitment as well as ingenuity.

5.4 *Backcasting*: The search for safe alternatives

All planning involves recognizing some goal, or goals, and adjusting system performance, or the system itself, to reach these goals. However, the perspective from which we approach the planning effort can have a huge impact on its effectiveness. As we have shown, incremental approaches based solely on look-ahead methods can create risk dilemmas rather than help avoid them. Effective high-stakes risk policy requires us to look back from goals and make our plans for progress accordingly. In this way, risk dilemmas can be avoided.

A scenario approach which takes as its basis a backward look from desirable futures is known as *backcasting*. Backcasting entails working backward from goals, say, a specified natural risk level, to identify proper system functioning within these parameters (see Figure 5.2). The goals reside in what we expect the desired future to look like. In high-stakes risk planning and control, this means reducing and maintaining risk at a naturally low level. By understanding the goals and parameters ahead of time, we avoid future dilemmas by reviewing suitable alternatives (including avoidance) early on in the planning process. This approach conforms to

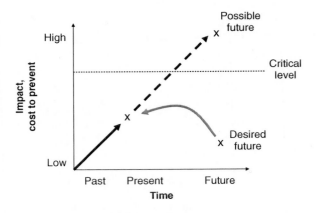

Figure 5.2   The basics of backcasting

the essence of what we have referred to as "preaction". It works to achieve sensible action *before* risks become entrenched.

Backcasting is a form of scenario analysis, in that it identifies plausible candidates for the future. Rather than emphasize adjustment to some plausible pathway by looking at past trends, themselves based on entrenched meta-goals, backcasting provides genuine alternative scenarios for achieving desired results. These scenarios are based on a response to well-articulated, transparent goals judged consistent with the wider, natural world order. Most forward looking scenario planning promotes the idea of incremental change, without providing substantive guidance for the control process. Forward looking plans often remain just that, plans, as opposed to true instruments of change. Backcasting at once makes our desires explicit, and suggests that to prepare for the future, we need to take appropriate action today.

In a purely mathematical setting, inverting the system model, that is, working from desired outputs to inputs rather than vice versa, will determine proper control actions ahead of time. Inversion lies at the root of the formal control process known as *feedforward*. In this setting, working the model forward or backward should produce identical results. A fully developed backcast works by not only reversing the process of planning from goal to output, but by looking at goals first and then looking at a spectrum of alternatives to achieve safe progress. This provides a more holistic look at just what should be changed, and how. It assumes that while our wider world system may be fixed (we can not change the laws of physics, for example), our social, economic, and technological subsystems can adjust. By examining possible courses of action before committing ourselves to a control policy, we avoid future problems, making it a *fail safe* option. That is, if we can't determine a safe pathway for some process or action then we don't take the action. Acceptable scenarios are those that are consistent with safe progress. Our scientific skill enters in making sure this set of responses is not empty.

Backcasting also changes the way we look at goals. By separating the goal-setting process, both temporally and conceptually, we reduce the influence of the past and the present on the goals themselves. So instead of identifying safety goals in terms of current system structures, or structures that might directly evolve in the future (based on extrapolations from past trends), we are free to express goals unencumbered by current constraints. The challenge then becomes overcoming these constraints if achieving the wider purpose dictates so. Instead of establishing goals and plans based on the tyranny of an entrenched past, we are able to exercise a freedom of choice based simply on the desirability of futures. This desirability is also now free to be influenced by the things that really mater, including an unfettered perspective on our natural place in the world.

Once again, this simple change in perspective can have an enormous impact on identifying, and implementing, safe pathways to progress that avoid risk dilemmas in the long run.

Last but not least, backcasting can result in a more participative structure for assessing and achieving goals. By making the goal-setting process explicit and unique, it makes obvious the need for all stakeholders to participate in defining these goals. In feedforward planning approaches, goals, like past trends, can become entrenched in the process, and therefore less transparent. Driven by past trends, the goals themselves may pander to an entrenched infrastructure. Hydrocarbon fuel mileage standards, for example, assume a hydrocarbon infrastructure. Without open discussion of the appropriateness of the goal, in light of a wider perspective on where we want to be with respect to both resource preservation and the risks of pollution in our automobile example, goals may themselves become entrenched in the process.

Of course, a holistic view of safety planning suggests that a realistic approach need not exclude feedback. Some element of feedback, based on forecasting from past events, is critical to keep short-run elements of the plan on track. The complete system of planning therefore behaves as a combined feedforward/feedback system, guided by backcasting from desired outcomes to feasible action plans. We can view backcasting as higher-level (long-run), while feedback provides lower-level (short-run) control. Systems engineers refer to such combinations of feedback and feedforward control as *cascaded* control. Understanding the proper place of statistical feedback and long-range feedforward control of existential risks is a key element of modern risk management.

5.5 Backcasting as exploratory modeling

Effective backcasting requires that uncertainty be captured through the evaluation of multiple plausible paths for goal achievement. Identifying and exploiting multiple plausible paths relates to the idea of *exploratory modeling*. Exploratory models are based on an ensemble of possible outcomes, bounded by plausibility. Exploratory models can be contrasted with traditional models that ignore uncertainty by combining observational and theoretical evidence into a single, consolidated model. In the process of consolidation, we loose valuable information about the uncertainties involved. Exploratory models preserve model uncertainty.

The backcasting process is about modeling pathways to safe progress under conditions of extreme uncertainty. The basis for this process is the requirement that we maintain some naturally low level of risk. Within this constraint, we are free to explore alternative avenues for its achievement. The result is an ensemble of possible safe courses of action whose envelope describes a fuzzy, yet useful, pathway into the future.

The uncertainty inherent in exploratory ensembles appears as the fuzzy intervals of possibility. These intervals form the envelope of exploratory results. The inherently fuzzy nature of exploratory modeling means that we need to assess and develop backcasting models in a more creative fashion. It is not just a matter of working possible precise models backward (i.e., inverting them). In fact, exploratory modeling owes more to the creative process of discovery than to the process of inductive verification or logical deduction. As such, it depends on novel ways to approach the problem. As a result, its back-looking approach, couched with respect to uncertain possibilities, can help place a better perspective on actions that can ultimately have catastrophic consequences.

5.6   Keeping our options open

The key to backcasting is not to identify one precise model of progress, but rather multiple plausible models. Dealing with the ensemble of options on this basis can improve the resilience of our models to uncertainties as well. By incorporating information from all these models we develop a *robust* approach to desired goals. In effect, exploration allows us to *keep our options open*. Doing so obviously requires us to forgo paths that may commit us to irreversible paths toward disaster. Flexibility under uncertainty means that certain paths that restrict flexibility, yet may offer obvious immediate benefits, may have to be forgone.

The notion of flexibility has long been a component of business and public strategy. We propose that under extreme uncertainty about catastrophic outcomes that flexibility proceeds under a survival constraint. That is, no prospective path can violate the natural risk threshold. Our challenge becomes designing pathways consistent with flexibility, yet respectful of the survival constraint.

Exploratory modeling lets us flesh out the uncertainty inherent in alternate paths, and take appropriate action. The extremes of these models of potential progress define our fuzzy boundaries for risk growth. Once we identify these boundaries, we can set appropriately precautionary strategies that respond to them. In this way uncertainty becomes part of the decision-making process, rather than an ancillary consideration. By simply relegating uncertainty to the list of trifles to be dealt with later on in the process, we invariably find ourselves faced with risk dilemmas down the road.

5.7 Planning, control and the meta-perspective

The theory of planning and control of complex systems took a large step in the immediate post-World War II era, with the introduction of the concept of *cybernetics*, or the control and organization of complex, dynamic systems. The rise of cybernetics paralleled interest in building a general theory of complex, interactive systems. Both the ideas of feedback and feedforward planning and control for achieving system goals in complex environments have been developed through the years, originally for mechanistic ("engineered") systems, and subsequently with application to biological, economic, and social systems. Management of risk on both a feedback and feedforward basis, including our notions of backcasting, can be viewed as a variant of cybernetic theory.

With the increased application of cybernetic ideas to social and economic systems, concern grew over the model-centered notion of both the system and its goals. While goals were often thought to be the most straightforward part of the system, and in the cases of machine control at least they are, the goals of living systems proved more difficult to articulate within traditional cybernetic models. As a result, a *second-order, or meta, theory of cybernetics* developed. Second-order cybernetics is the study of *why* we control, not just how we control. The second-order emphasis is a way to introduce the idea of teleology or purpose into system study. Rather than concentrating on system goals, and how to achieve them, the teleological approach aims at understanding a deeper purpose of both the controller *and* what is to be controlled (and why). An understanding of purpose can, in turn, have an effect on our understanding of immediate goals, the system, the planning and control mechanisms applied, and even how we understand the outcomes or outputs of our system. The wider

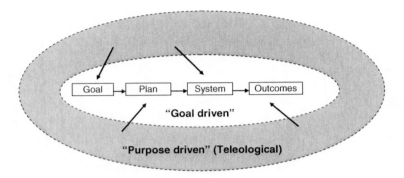

Figure 5.3 "Second-order", or meta-, planning

or encapsulating approach of second-order cybernetics is shown in Figure 5.3.

A backcasting analysis is ideally suited toward capturing this meta-view of planning and control. The approach operates at a level beyond consolidated models, into one that includes plausible ensembles. With the benefit of looking backward toward potential systems, we are given the opportunity, theoretically at least, not only to mold how we plan and control these systems, but also to plan the structure of the systems themselves. Separating the goal-setting phase from the immediate also helps us understand how any particular system and plan fit into the wider purpose of the world. By making desired futures more explicit, we are also committed to understanding *why* these futures are desired. A proper backcasting exercise must necessarily consider this wider purpose, or teleology. In the treatment of high-stakes risks, this brings up questions of existence, its value, and how we assure its achievement. As we have shown above, concentration on lower order goals alone, especially short-term ones, can obscure the wider picture. Backcasting therefore provides a genuinely holistic view of the planning process as it relates to our wider purpose in nature.

It is this meta-view that ultimately reconciles the actions of planning and control with the idea that our fate is prescribed in the inevitable order of the wider natural world, or cosmos. Evolution favors those that are so prepared. Our goal then in planning is not coercive, not manipulative, but rather to set the stage for the unfettered flow of evolution. On this view it is mere acquiescence to risk that is coercive – we are forced into an unnatural order. And for what?

Further reading

The defects of the identify–assess–treat model of risk assessment and management with respect to high-stakes risk management, and the importance of assessing safe alternatives early on in the process of planning process as an essential precondition to effective precaution, are outlined in *Making Better Environmental Decisions: An Alternative to Risk Assessments* (MIT Press, 2000), by Mary O'Brien.

Backcasting is increasingly recognized as a cogent approach for identifying and implementing safe alternatives. For more on the theory and application of backcasting from desirable futures to safe alternatives, see Karl-Henrich Dreborg's "Essence of Backcasting", *Futures*, December 1996. Analysts concerned about our world's dependence on hydrocarbon energy sources were the first to use formalized backcasting techniques. For example, Amory Lovin's *Soft Energy Paths* (Ballinger, 1977) backcasts from a safer, petroleum-independent future to determine sustainable energy alternatives. The approach was subsequently developed into a general concept for advanced scenario modeling in1982 by J. B. Robinson in "Energy Backcasting: A Proposed Method of Policy Analysis", which appeared in a 1982 issue of the journal *Energy Policy*. For an overview and modern history of the backcasting technique, see Jaco Quist's *Backcasting for a Sustainable Future: The Impact After 10 Years* (Eburon Academic Publishers, 2007). Precursors of the backcasting approach include economist Adolph Lowe's concept of *instrumental analysis* which linked planning efforts to working backward from desired policy outcomes (see his *On Economic Knowledge: Toward a Science of Political Economics* [Harper & Row, 1965]).

On the use of exploratory modeling to help cope with uncertainty in complex models, see Stephan Bankes' "Exploratory Modeling for Policy analysis", *Operations Research*, 41 (3), 1993. On the related concept of robustness ("keeping your options open"), see *Rational Analysis for a Problematic World*, by Johnathan Rosenhead (Wiley, 2001).

Early cybernetic thought viewed human systems as analogs of mechanical system, as in, for example, Norbert Wiener's *The Human Use of Human Beings: Cybernetics and Society* (Doubleday, 1954). Criticisms of this mechanical approach led to the recognition that the proper study of planning and control mechanisms in human society is not always about the process of planning, but also how we *plan the process*. The result was the rise of a "second-order" cybernetics that recognizes the importance of human purpose in the process of planning, as outlined, for example, in the work of systems scientists such as Heinz von Foerster, in *Cybernetics of Cybernetics* (University of Illinois, 1974).

6
Risk Planning on a Wider Scale

In the previous chapters we have identified the nature of high-stakes risks as widespread, and accumulative. Their uncertain character, combined with the finality of their outcomes, requires a strong precautionary approach. From this basic nature of high-stakes risk, we can easily figure that some sort of planning effort is essential. We have framed this basic structure for assessing alternatives for safe progress using the scenario-based structure known as backcasting. In backcasting, we attempt to identify feasible paths of safe progress, which at the same time maintain some degree of flexibility against the unknown. The very notions of widespread effects and identification of desirable end-states means that any such efforts can only succeed if applied on a wider scale.

We have also noted in the previous chapters the dangers of an incremental approach to high-stakes risks. Theoretically, piecemeal identification and planning for risk can create serious gaps in our understanding of the risks we face, leading to the creeping phenomenon of risk dilemmas – we become doomed if we do, doomed if we don't. Practically, selective approaches based on the regulation of risk on a permissive basis, within the market system, have arguably made our world less safe rather than more. The corrective action we would suggest here is some sort of coordinated planning effort for a safer future, applied on a social scale. Such coordination itself presumes some infrastructure for planning exists, or can be constructed. In this chapter we provide some suggestions for wider scale planning that fit the characteristics of high-stakes risk management previously identified.

6.1 The problem of permissive regulation

The most prominent public response to high-stakes risks today occurs under some form of regulation. Regulation involves the use of governmental legislations, rules, and legal structures to implement a cogent risk management plan, with societal goals in mind. Regulation may act to influence actions of the producing and consuming public through modifying the market, for example, in terms of taxes or subsidies, or via direct prohibition.

Such structures, however, offer only a very imperfect method of coordination of risk goals. As a result, those precautionary efforts that have existed in the past have been doomed to failure due to post-fact application within such regulatory structures. In addition, uncoordinated applications that work within an otherwise "free" market structure, either through direct prohibitions or restrictions, or via attempts to alter the market structure itself (e.g., taxes and subsidies), are themselves subject to subversion in the name of goals of the prevailing economic system.

When such market structures prevail, regulatory approaches are often rendered ineffective through various forms of subversion. Among them, the attempts to frustrate any such efforts on the basis of appeals through a legal system itself geared toward the demands of a market economy. As a result, all regulatory systems are subject to some degree of *capture*, or co-option, of their activities by special interests. The application of easily manipulated cost/benefit analysis is a case in point. Although regulation did not directly cause our current state with respect to high-stakes risk, and while it has made some inroads into a truly precautionary mode of high-stakes management, our review of the current state of the world suggests that, in general, modern regulatory regimes have failed us with regard to making the world safer for all its inhabitants.

In this atmosphere, regulations can only function as a quasi-control mechanism that simply cannot achieve a true regulative function. The results only frustrate both the regulators and those regulated, with little ultimate effect on overall risk levels. The basic problem with regulation today is that it is often inhibited to operate within the zone of statistical risk. We have shown in the previous chapters that if we want to avoid catastrophe, we need to establish some minimum acceptable risk level, based on the *practical* impossibility of calamity. At the very least, this involves maintaining a level of catastrophic risk, that is at or below some natural level, recognizing the inherent uncertainties involved.

More often that not, these uncertainties are large enough to require some sort of gap or safety cushion between observable and unobservable risks. Maintaining a natural safety cushion requires maintaining a separation between the natural risk threshold, or what we might call the *de minimis* level, and that level at which risk becomes statistically apparent, also known as the *de manifestis* level. The de minimis level might be given a fuzzy interpretation as being somewhere around the proverbial "one in a million" annual probability of disaster. The de manifestis level in many industrialized countries is often set as high, one chance in a thousand (as is the case with workplace safety regulation in the United States). The region in between de manifestis and de minimis becomes especially critical when (1) we are dealing with events whose probability can only be assessed very imperfectly, making precise identification of risk difficult, if not impossible; and (2) we don't get a second chance to make the right choice (the *catastrophe problem*).

The permissive attitude in risk regulation, as opposed to its precautionary alternative, is often expressed in the form of *risk tolerability criteria*. In effect, tolerability represents a quasi-cost/benefit structure. We aim for the de minimis level, unless benefits (alternatively, costs) are too high (see Figure 6.1). The criteria remain genuinely restrictive only with respect to the high-end, or the de manifestis level. Of course, given the uncertainties involved, "one in a thousand" may be very difficult to distinguish from "one in a hundred", and that puts us at or over the de manifestis level.

The permissive structure of regulation is meant to take on a reassuring character by promoting the idea that we

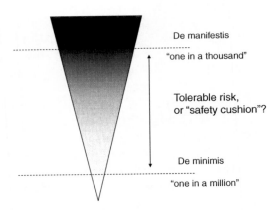

Figure 6.1 Tolerable risk criterion (adapted from the UK Health and Safety Executives Guidelines, *The Tolerability of Risk*, published by the Health and Safety Executive of the UK [HSE Books, 2001])

are doing our best, avoiding at least the most visible of risks. Again, any such statistical analysis is not suited to catastrophic risk problems. The potential for very large losses cannot be averaged out over any reasonable time horizon. As a result, the typical cost/benefit proceeds from desired outcome ("accept the risk") to adjustment of costs and benefits. To make the criteria fit the conclusions costs are invariably understated, benefits overstated, or both. The goal of regulatory risk management does not support catastrophic risk avoidance, but rather the charge of unfettered technological progress, whose motto is that if we can do it, we should.

Focusing on what we can observe, statistically, is about observing only the tip of the iceberg of risk. We are supposed to take great comfort as statistical levels of risk are shown to be reduced, which says absolutely nothing about the large-scale risks that are effectively hidden below the point of observation (in terms of *average* outcomes). We navigate this statistical regulatory path at the brink of catastrophe only at great peril, not only due to the threat of what lies below, but also due to the imperviousness of the permissive regulatory approach to trying to *find out* what those threats may entail.

6.2 Coordination on a social scale

Regulatory responses to risk that work within existing market systems offer a piecemeal, incremental approach to dealing with risk that is ultimately ineffective, or at best marginally effective. Permissive regulatory schemes, and the economic and social structures that support them, subject us to the full uncertainty of high-stakes risk accumulation. We rush headlong into risk, and hope for the best. Given the atmosphere of uncertainty that surrounds complex risk processes, the approach is bound to be ineffective.

The nature of high-stakes risk demands that we both identify the often integrated potentials for dangerous risk, and make the necessary decisions at a properly coordinated level. Risks that can grow, or combine, to affect an entire society, or the natural world itself, are unlikely to be tamed by concentrating simply on their individual origins, one at a time. At the most basic level, adequate treatment of high-stakes risk requires what we have referred to as a *philosophy of risk*. For any philosophy to be effective it needs to be applied on a consistent basis.

Beyond agreement on an appropriate philosophy of risk, we need mechanisms to enforce the uniform and effective treatment of chance events with possible high-stakes outcomes. The idea that some moral philosophy of risk will work through universal ascension of the affected group, and some sort of spontaneous reversion thereto, does not seem theoretically or practically supportable. Practically, a moralist position that calls upon individuals to change their attitudes toward risk, and thereby change our collective psyche with respect to risk accumulation, has simply not worked in the past. If, for no other reason, there are strong counter forces at work which seek to win the hearts and minds of individuals. The existence of powerful groups with a self-interest in preserving that power have the ability to subvert the effort, or at least muddle it to the point of inaction.

The sensitivity of the components of large economic and social systems suggests that expecting that the proper coordination of risk will appear spontaneously, through voluntary actions of its constituents (via free market incentives, or otherwise), is simply too incredible a vision. The notion of some automatic reversion to a proper course for risk is the hope of most that hold a strictly moral position with respect to risk, as well as those who support individualized cost/benefit approach based on a narrowly focused utilitarianism. These approaches sustain incrementalism, and a faith in the status quo (the *best possible world* option). A radical rethinking of risk requires that it should be tackled on its most basic level, that of social and economic institutions. Adequately dealing with the high-stakes risk we face is not just about changing our way of *thinking*, it is about changing our way of *doing* things that may lead to irreversible risks.

Planning involves both the identification and control of large-scale systems on a coordinated basis. Often, planning proceeds on the basis of some model, or representation of the system, combined with agreed upon goals, as in the case of backcasting. We add the suggestion here that, to be successful, any such backcasting efforts need to be carried out on a basis that involves coordination by all those affected.

Even though coordinated planning of risk decisions has some logically appealing advantages, the question becomes how, and more specifically, at what level, can this coordination be achieved to best suit our purposes? The tradeoff is one of gaining sufficient generality, especially for tackling wide-scale, global risks, against the practicality of the system. Wide-scale planning on a centralized basis engenders not only issues of feasibility, but also the specter of large-scale risks from a system in which places all our safety eggs in a single basket, so to speak. On the other hand, small-scale systems are subject to a myopia that may further encourage piecemeal, incremental solutions that either ignore or are ineffective against wide-scale risks. One thing is for sure, the dispute over the proper way to plan can itself become a divisive diversion which promotes inaction. These are the issues we need to get out in the open, however, if we are to make planning for a safer future work.

6.3 Integrating risk planning with social and economic planning

Risk is an intertwined part of our social and economic lives. Given the basic criteria for risk planning of achieving an overall level of natural risk, it seems unlikely that a separate regime of risk planning can be carried out without some coordinated view of our social and economic perspective. The conclusion seems inescapable then that risk planning must occur *within some sort of architecture of coordinated economic and social planning.*

In fact, the process of risk planning we propose – a holistic view that emphasizes the assessment of specifications for a naturally risk-free society – is a simple adjunct to most conceptions of economic planning on a wider scale. For example, in both conceptions and articulations of past planned national economies, so-called *input–output models* have been used to reflect the relationships between components of the system. Systems of production that satisfy human wants and needs are segregated into their component parts, allowing planners to best assess alternatives to achieve production goals in satisfaction of these stated objectives. Natural risk goals could be easily integrated into these types of formal planning approaches.

The key to risk treatment in wider models of social and economic development is the transparency they provide. No longer are high-stakes risk elements treated as an afterthought, to be justified using a post-fact cost/benefit analysis. Now, risk becomes part of the economic planning process. The truly democratic nature of the process is reflected in the openness that risk issues now achieve. While difficult issues of choosing the *right* alternatives exist, by backcasting and preplanning accordingly we can hopefully avoid the type of entrenchment that leads to subsequent risk dilemmas. Should the specter of such dilemmas appear on the horizon, we can be assured that it could only be a result of some defect in our planning process, despite best efforts, and not based on some self-interested approach that attempts to disguise risk. It is this visibility which makes planned systems so different and, we would argue, superior to market systems in a truly democratic system of deciding our future.

The combination of risk planning with a system of economic planning not only has benefits in terms of expedience, but it also exploits some obvious synergies. As we have pointed out in our global risk assessments in the previous chapters, a considerable number of the high-stakes risks we face today, including those related directly to the functioning of the modern economy (e.g., recession and depression), issues of income inequality (which are driven by, and in turn drive, social issues), the exploitation of natural and human resources along with the political and social tensions, are related to the increasing uncertainty of technological risk exposures. The source of these social tensions from unequal exposures to risk may have resolutions more adequately confronted by social and economic planning systems. Issues of democratic rule may themselves be more susceptible to amicable and equitable solution within a planned system. This wider synergism must be considered when assessing the potential of wide-scale planning systems to create a safer, equitable, and just environment for both human and non-human life.

Less simple, from a practical perspective, is how such coordinated social and economic systems are to be implemented. The most basic issue remains one of feasibility in the face of the sheer scale of the decisions, in terms of both impacts and individuals involved. How do we implement such a large-scale system to function effectively in coordinating what could amount to millions of decisions? The notion of feasibility runs beyond sheer number of calculations, and involves question of knowledge. Can a planned system duplicate the distribution and dissemination of knowledge necessary for these systems to fulfill their basic functions (i.e., safely satisfying the wants and needs of society)? Failing to do so introduces the potential for negative side effects, or counter-risks, entailed by a centralized planning system which may itself face failure potentials from a variety of sources. One logical approach to feasibility is determining at what level identification, planning, and coordination should proceed.

6.4   Centralized, or decentralized?

At first glance, the notion of wide-scale control of societal risk may seem a remarkably daunting task. On an empirical basis, outcomes of planned economies have generally been negative. Comprehensive risk planning would entail no less scale, probably more. Is there really any hope for a planned solution to existential risks?

The failure and subsequent collapse of centrally planned economic and social systems in countries like the former Union of Soviet Socialist Republics (USSR) and China is frequently cited as evidence that such wide-scale planning is simply not feasible, and perhaps dangerous in and of itself. First of all, it is in fact debatable to what extent that planned economic systems could be called failures, at least with respect to their explicit (and implicit) goals. Among these, military and scientific superiority. For decades, both the USSR and China advanced under such systems, or at least advanced according to the planner's concept of progress, based on their narrow goals. That the concept of progress under such systems gained far from universal acceptance by its constituents is without a doubt. Both the USSR and China clearly sacrificed individual freedoms in an effort to achieve advances in science and military power. That issues other than planning and its alleged failures contributed to the demise of these political systems should be equally obvious.

Despite its complexities, some element of central, or centralized planning, is key to the successful functioning of every governmental, social, and economic function in the world today. Modern business thrives on planning mechanisms. Some of these businesses have larger annual economic outputs than many smaller countries. Public goods and services remain for the most part, even in "free market" countries such as the United States, planned based on central or centralized authority (with social input).

There is also the possibility that planned systems be implemented on a more directly decentralized, local level, with wider linkages as needed. Debates on the degree of centralization of economic planning, meaning how focused control is at the epicenter of control of the society itself, have existed since the dawn of modern political, economic, and social systems. In individualized, market-based systems, where varieties of trade between individuals determine economic (and to a great degree, social) life, no coordinating mechanism besides individual self-interest is involved. As we have shown in the previous chapters, some degree of public oversight might enter such systems, based on overarching social goals. We have generally referred to such interventions as regulation. The key is that the market system remains the primary background for all economic choices. All planning, on the other hand, involves a degree of direct control. The primary distinction is at what level specific decisions with regard to the functioning of the system should be made.

In contrast to centralized control, with some appointed social body (i.e., the *state*), less structured, communal structures have been suggested in various degrees throughout the history of modern social/economic planning discussions. A recent option appears in so-called *participatory economic systems*. Here, coordination is maintained based on well-specified social and economic goals. Specifying and carrying out these goals, however, is left decentralized, community units. The size of these units varies, but is most directly controlled by production relationships. That is, the scale of production necessary to satisfy public needs.

The question is whether such decentralized control could provide sufficiently wide coordination of goals to deal with societal issues, including risk. Many risk issues, just like more general economic ones, could of course be decentralized according to the regional scope of their impacts. In this way, for example, a local group may administer risk issues related to pollution by local industry (at least to the extent these pollutants do not stray beyond the community). The problem is that many risk issues are themselves global in scope, and these are arguably the most critical. To the extent we centralize control based on scope, it is clear that larger issues will once again be subject to the fragility of large-scale systems in the face of their own failure to perform as intended (for whatever reason).

In many cases, the distinction between centralized and decentralized planning blurs, with most social and economic systems having characteristics of both. The public education system in the United States is based on equal access to a quality primary and secondary education, and is essential to modern subsistence. Hierarchical control is achieved through a series of somewhat "low tech" communications. The result is often a remarkable coordination of educational goals on a nationwide basis, though inequalities in wealth still serve to stifle the system. Other subsistence-based planning systems around the world include healthcare, housing, transportation, and the provision of food. Given the essential nature of many of these products and services, it is unlikely that advanced planning systems, such as those that rely on electronic computers, are absolutely necessary for their functioning (the US educational system being a case in point). This suggests that at least our basic subsistence needs are amenable to some form of cogent planning. The key is the promulgation of social goals, consistent with a wider view of our place in the natural world, rather than control via specialized self-interests.

Empirically, all advanced economies today function as hybrids, or mixed economies, consisting of elements of social planning, market systems, and regulation. The larger question becomes at what level of centralization can incrementalism be overcome. That is, what level of control is necessary to make changes that can genuinely affect the outcomes? We can, of course, seek to establish this level experimentally. The danger is that in the time it takes us to find a solution, it may be too late. Observations of evolutionary history suggest that sometimes it takes big jumps to set us on the right track. A radical rethinking is along the lines of one of these large leaps.

6.5 The first step: Evaluating risk on a societal basis

We may not be able to identify today precise answers to how control of risk may be best achieved. We can, however, infer some logical starting points. Among them, the realization that the most basic precondition for any sort of rational preplanning is an understanding, however vague, of the risks we face. This understanding needs to be placed first and foremost on a coordinated footing. This would suggest that, at the very least, our *evaluations* of the high-stakes risks we face be placed on a social level. For example, such coordination may take the form of a national committee or format for the identification of risks on a uniform basis, and the application of risk criteria in uniformity as well. Only under these conditions can systematic planning, at any level, begin.

A basic building block of economics is individual businesses. Business organizations have comprehensive risk management departments, and so should larger, social entities. These businesses recognize the need to coordinate overall risk into a risk strategy, which is underneath guided by a risk philosophy (however self-centered they may be). Coordinated by a common risk management vision, businesses in this way find ways to flourish in a world of uncertainties. That model needs to be, and can be, applied on a social basis as well.

Coordinating risk assessment on a wider societal level has side benefits as well. Such risk assessments can and should become part of a wider evaluation of our technological and scientific future that includes assessment of viability and proper investment potential (both public and private). Once again, modern business enterprise benefits from a coordination of technological planning efforts, often outside of the system of market forces that coordinates exchange. Likewise, countries around the world have recognized the importance of a coordinated plan for technology assessment and deployment to further both economic and social goals. These efforts can and should go hand in hand with wider risk assessment efforts.

Of course, we need to recognize that merely placing our understanding of risk on a wider basis does not in and of itself translate to effective implementation. It is only a first step. Recognition remains consistent with incremental arguments, and transitions based on voluntary moral commitments. As we have argued in the previous chapters, to expect such commitments to gel spontaneously, perhaps prodded by the greater degree of knowledge such coordinated recognition provides, is not a realistic position. And, there is nothing about market systems that suggests that enough coordination on risk reduction would be forthcoming fast enough (if at all). Once we recognize the primacy of planning, the problem becomes one of implementation on a coordinated, definitive basis. However, if we accept the fuzzy nature of accumulating risk potentials as reasonable representation of the real-world, we have no choice but to plan against disaster.

Further reading

While there are many writings on risk regulation, few recognize the true complexities and unique nature of high-stakes risks. For more on the complications of regulating such risks, including the danger of regulating to "statistical" levels, see *Normal Accidents: Living with High Risk Technologies* (Princeton University Press, 1999), by Charles Perrow.

The "capture" of regulation by powerful special interests (essentially, those regulated) has long been an issue in the study of modern business regulation. See, for example, *Social Responsibility and the Business Predicament: Studies in the Regulation of Economic Activity*, edited by James W. McKie for The Brookings Institution (1974). The impact of vested interests on retarding environmental regulations, for example, is explored in Douglas Booth's "Economic Growth and the Limits of Environmental Regulation: A Social Economic Analysis", published in the *Review of Social Economy* (Winter, 1995).

On the wider conception of social and economic planning for complex social and economic systems, from a modern perspective, see Franco Archibugi's *Planning Theory: From the Political Debate to the Methodological Reconstruction* (Springer, 2008). Archibugi introduces a general theory of planning for progress, which he refers to as *planology*.

For more on the ideas and applications of centralized economic planning, see *Alternative Approaches to Economic*

Planning (St. Martin's, 1981), by Martin Cave and Paul Hare. A seminal reference on the distinction between regulation and planning in the social/economic sphere is K. William Kapp's "Economic Regulation and Economic Planning: A Theoretical Classification of Different Types of Economic Control", *American Economic Review* (December 1939), reprinted (partially) in H. B. Summers and R. E. Summers, *Increasing Federal Power* (H.W. Wilson, 1940).

Michael Albert outlines a participatory structure, with decentralized planning, in *Parecon: Life After Capitalism* (Verso, 2004). The author attempts to develop a wider social and economic system that goes beyond the defects of capitalist market systems, yet avoids the state excesses and inefficiencies that have been typical of previous centralized planning regimes.

For a reasoned alternative that combines centralized and decentralized aspect of planning, while avoiding the essentially status quo position entailed by quasi-regulated markets, see Boris Frankel, *The Post-Industrial Utopians* (University of Wisconsin Press, 1987). Frankel comes to his position after analyzing the failures of market programs, and synthesizing the positions of those that would seek a better way, both in terms of centralized and decentralized options for socialized control.

The economist K. William Kapp was an early champion of coordinated risk planning on a social and economic basis. He discusses the steps toward more comprehensive risk planning, including coordinated risk assessment, from the standpoint of environmental risks in his various works as collected in *Social Costs, Economic Development, and Environmental Disruption* (University Press of America, 1983), edited by John E. Ullmann. See especially Chapter 8, "Governmental Furtherance of Environmentally Sound Technologies as a Focus of Research and Environmental Policies", where he furthers the idea of an *innovative branch* of government that assesses proposals for alternative (safe) futures.

7
Is a Safer World "Worth It"?

We have offered here an expanded approach to planning for safe progress, based on the notion of preserving natural levels of risk. Although the pathways to safe progress have yet to be determined, any approach to preplanning for risk will require some radical changes to the way we live, and indeed our whole system of living. Only in this way can we avoid risk dilemmas of the "doomed if we do, doomed if we don't" variety. Identifying and establishing wider systems of risk planning and control will undoubtedly require great effort. So while even though the means may eventually come into clearer focus, the bigger question becomes one of valuation. Is pursuing the effort to achieve a safer world "worth it"?

The problem is that many forms of traditional risk assessment, including those based on simplistic, post-fact cost/benefit comparisons, take a very slanted view of costs. As we have seen, this view can get us into risk dilemmas, rather than help resolve them. To understand the value of a more precautionary stance toward high-stakes risks, we need to understand the deeper nature of costs, and how they fit into the balance of life. Once we gain this understanding, we need to effectively incorporate these wider goals into our process of decision.

7.1   Recognizing the true costs of progress

Most risk analysts view risk as a cost. We trade off risks to achieve progress. Yet, when the tradeoff involves life or health, or the health of our environment, the resulting bargain becomes complicated, perhaps even meaningless. In economics, which we define as the study of how we produce, distribute, and consume the products and services that promote life, we often rely on the *market system* of supply and demand to balance our desires with the costs of achieving them. Economic costs in this system are viewed as tradeoffs among resources for achieving consumption goals. Crucial to the market view of economics, and underlying the need to make tradeoffs, is the notion of *scarcity*. Relative scarcity of resources demands that we pick and choose their combination so as to maximize satisfaction (utility) at minimum cost. Money provides a convenient medium for expressing these tradeoffs among the many choices.

Yet can we properly consider our life and health, and that of our wider natural environment, as tradable goods? Even in classic economic analysis, scarcity is always a short-run phenomenon. It is something to be overcome either through innovation or by living a life in which our wants and desires are in some way limited: Satiable rather than insatiable. Only in a world that wants more and more is scarcity a genuine problem, a real constraint, in the words of the economists.

Economics offers a vehicle for the analysis of these tradeoffs, all in the spirit of balancing costs against benefits in a world of scarcity. We can look at this tradeoff functioning in terms of the idea of supply and demand, as shown in Figure 7.1. We show here the supply and demand for some "risk-inducing" product or activity. Demand is determined by consumers who want to optimize satisfaction of this product, service, or activity.

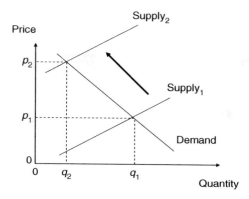

Figure 7.1   Adjusting values ("price") in the market model

On the other hand, supply, or output, is determined by the costs of production, and the producers' desire to maximize individual profits. We begin with the initial assumption that an equilibrium, or balance, exists between suppliers and demanders, at quantity q_1 and price p_1, as noted on the graph.

How, then, are the costs of risks assimilated? When the cost of risk can be treated in a statistical fashion, we simply add the expected, or average, value into our other production costs. Should the initial analysis fail to capture the deleterious effects of, say, product-related pollution on our health and the health of the environment, we simply *internalize* these external costs. That is, we add them to our already recognized production costs. This recognition of the increase in true costs may be voluntary, but more likely driven through some sort of government or public intervention. For example, external cost may be internalized through some sort of tax, or via mandatory insurance. In terms of our market analysis, doing so reduces the supply at each price level (due to higher costs). However, just as in the case of cost/benefit analysis, post-fact application of this cost adjustment could carry risks of its own. At the most basic economic level, it will increase the price of the product. This, in turn, could cause greater economic hardships, which may themselves translate into bad physical effects. As in the case of cost/benefit analysis, we now find that post-fact valuation has resulted in a risk dilemma. While the market model can be made to recognize these effects, there is no solution to be had to these dilemmas within the model itself. No amount of static economic analysis will help us get out of risk dilemmas once we get into them. We have suggested, on the other hand, that such dilemmas could be avoided by suitable *preaction*. So, like cost/benefit analysis, an inadequate economic analysis in public policy with respect to high-stakes risks is easily subverted into acting as a prop, or artifice, which can be (ab)used by those who might seek to misguide and misdirect our attention from what really matters. Distorted values are imposed, and the perpetrators can only hope that the public does not notice the distortion. The analysis is meant to look more scientific by dressing it up in the garb of classical economics (here, "supply and demand"). Once again, we have to recognize that it's not the system itself that distorts our perceptions, it's the way the system promulgates values through the decision process.

In fact, forcing the market to internalize external costs doesn't make sense. It's not part of the make-up of the market to do so. Individualized profit maximization is about finding ways to get around internalization. A change in the way that such competition for scarce resources, in the *relative* sense, cannot be forced by regulation in a market economy. As we have suggested above, attempts to do so have failed throughout the history of modern market systems. We might reasonably argue, once again, *that it is this very market system that got us to where we are today*. These observations suggest that

this system does not accurately reflect our moral require-
ments, as, say, outlined in Kant's categorical imperative.
Forcing it to do so causes more problems than it solves.

A further defect in the market system is that it lacks
the dynamics necessary to determine adequate solutions
to high-stakes risks. At best, the market provides for simple feedback control. Incremental adjustments are made,
based on observed deviations from plan. In this way, the
market is perfectly suitable to statistical risk decisions,
and frequently acts as a reasonable basis for monetizing
such decisions (within the identify–assess–treat, or I-A-T,
model of risk management). As we have shown above,
the key to avoiding risk dilemmas is understanding the
dynamic nature of risk. The economic theory of markets
does not include an adequate theory of dynamics. As
such, it hides rather than accentuates the potential for
disaster inherent in many of its choices.

At its root, the market system is guided by the
static view inherent in a very short-sighted utilitarian
approach, which suggests all production is about maximizing monetary profits. This system is inadequate to
capture our notion of natural values. The simple fact
is that business firms would hold back an innovation,
thereby reducing safety, *if they could increase profit by
doing so*. By ignoring true costs in favor immediate
benefits the general public is induced into the classic
bait-and-switch fraud. We are baited with the promise
of some ideal life, as risk growth is obscured by a fundamentally static economic theory of response. We eventually find ourselves switched from the promised land of
abundance to a very unseemly world in which the lure
of the good life has been replaced with living under the
threat of disaster.

Despite the lip-service it pays to scarcity, this classical approach to economic valuation is about nothing
more than achieving the outward trappings of progress,

in terms of continued output growth. Maximum profits are the fuel for further increase in growth, as reflected in the economy's money denominated sum of output – its gross domestic product, or GDP. The notions of scarcity and the tradeoffs it engenders become merely scapegoats for why we are unable to produce a safer world, despite these outward signs of progress... because it would "cost too much".

7.2 Moral absolutes as infinite values

Moral absolutes are created when we take our existence seriously. As such, they can only be incorporated into a purely utilitarian system by setting these utilitarian values high enough. That is, when the utilitarian values are set at, or near, infinity, properly reflecting their absolute character. Once we make the proper adjustments, however, the precautionary approach and cost/benefit in terms of market valuations coincide. Therefore, by properly valuing results, we make any decision theory naturally more precautionary. The alleged distinction between precautionary and economic cost/benefit in this sense may be overstated by critics on both sides of the debate. The real distinction is how, and how well, absolute notions of moral value are captured, and when. The value of the precautionary principle, as a principle of decision exclusive to high-stakes risk, is that it makes the notion of absolute, or at least very high, valuation of our natural moral commitments perfectly plain.

We may reason, then, that in light of the need to maintain balance, a greater constancy of decisions in the sense of maintaining our commitment to moral absolutes is gained by *subordinating the idea of monetary valuation*. In this setting, prohibitions act as absolute constraints. Monetary cost/benefit becomes just one component of an extended realm of choice.

One way of extending important value-based decisions in this way is through the use of *multi-criteria decision-making (MCDM)* techniques. In a multi-criteria framework, when threats to survival exist, precautionary avoidance acts as an inviolable restriction. On the other hand, where a monetary market evaluation may be suitable, for example, in the domain of statistical risks with moderate outcomes (i.e., typical market transactions), it is retained.

Multi-criteria decision-making can in this way become a critical component of a planning process aimed at achieving and maintaining balance. First of all, it helps articulate the criteria of decision as part of a participatory process of identifying goals. Setting goals on a recognized multi-criteria basis means that all criteria must be adequately identified, by all involved. This helps us cull out hidden agendas, based on self-interest. The analysis aims at understanding all the concerns of the public affected, and making sure they are adequately captured in the analysis. Rather than be treated as an aberration within a market valuation process, absolutes achieve their full import in the multi-criteria process. The multi-criteria approach also makes the effects of absolutes (i.e., absolute constraints) on behavior clear. This helps enforcement by the appropriate authority. Last but not least, the constraints-based approach integrates our technical notion of the avoidance of unnatural risks (i.e., the *danger zone*) and the uncertainties they engender into the wider valuation process.

Many people view modern business corporations as well-honed decision-makers, at least within their sphere of interest. In fact, many business decisions are made on a multi-criteria basis. So even though profit maximization is a crucial criterion for decision, the most fundamental goal for most corporations is *survival*. On a multi-criteria basis, the profit maximization goal is applied only after its survival constraint is satisfied. This survival goal is reflected in a variety of financial decision rules, known as *safety first* principles. In this sense, corporations are precautionary with respect to their own financial interests. Faced with risks to their own existence, these businesses rely on risk management strategies that include the legal protections under the corporate form of organization itself, the use of insurance to protect against the negative financial results of a variety of physical perils, and various government protections. As a result, data shows that the typical business corporation in the United States has an annual likelihood of financial failure *below* that of the fatality rate of the average citizen (i.e., the average US corporation has a better chance of surviving the year than most of its workers do).

Recognizing the true underlying costs in this fashion makes economic cost/benefit no more resilient to risk dilemmas than minimax-based precaution. The only way that economic cost/benefit can be made to appear to avoid the dilemmas is by *undervaluing* the true costs (i.e., failing to internalize critical externalities).

7.3   Achieving a natural balance

The issue of proper action in the face of threats to survival once again reverts to designing ways to *avoid* risk dilemmas, early on in the process of planning for progress. As we have shown above, a wider planning for naturally risk-free alternatives can be made feasible. A vestige of the economic approach is trying to identify what we must give up to achieve a naturally risk-free life. The real issue, in light of the moral issues that underlie the question of survival, is rather one of *continuity*, not tradeoffs. Adopting the *preactionary* view to avoiding the forced choices that result from risk dilemmas means that we need to take a wider view of valuation in the economic setting. We also need an approach to existential decisions that respects the need for such holistic planning. In achieving an economics compatible with the survival ethic, we need to replace the ideas of scarcity and tradeoffs with that of a natural *continuity* of resources. This continuity, in turn, implies a balance of resource use and renewal. Balance in this sense involves the idea of equipoise, rather than tradeoff. This balance involves harmony in goals and purpose, not competition among them.

So while the economist notion of tradeoffs is based on the threat of scarcity, the economist deals with relative scarcity, not scarcity in its absolute sense. We are given some set production abilities in wheat and steel, for example, with a given amount of resources to be devoted to producing these two goods. Resources are limited at any point in time, so we need to decide how to best utilize them. This results in choices based on a tradeoff in the production of steel for wheat and vice versa. The more steel we produce, the less wheat. The relationship is formalized in what the economist calls the *production possibilities curve*. Like most analysis in economics, this tradeoff analysis is static, both in terms of time and other critical variables, such as consumer wants and needs. In fact, the production possibilities curve can move outward with the advance of technology. That is, we might innovate so as to produce more steel and wheat. Likewise, static consumer preferences may become variable, as when we assume that some degree of satiety can be obtained at perhaps some lower level of steel and wheat production, say through a change in lifestyles, or a decrease in population.

On an absolute scale then, when the wider world and its goals must be considered in a dynamic fashion, the notion of relative scarcity becomes insignificant. The wider question becomes whether we can achieve our wants and desires, including freedom from risks, in this framework. In what ways can we combine effective use of technology and a suitable lifestyle so as to satisfy our desire for progress while at the same time so doing so *safely*? The choice cannot be put in the same terms as those involving simple consumer goods.

Valuation from the absolute standpoint is related to achieving a harmony, or a symbiosis, with the natural world (in the wider sense of *cosmos*, as we have described above) and the resources it offers us. This implies we may find ourselves out of balance from time to time, for whatever reasons. Re-establishing this balance, however, is not about tradeoffs of costs for benefits. It is not a matter of exchange, but rather a matter of pure adjustments of forces. To understand the true nature of safety, we must understand that we don't really "give up" things to achieve safety. Instead, we make safety a part of our natural conception of progress. If some action involves serious risks, we don't take it. In the process, balance is maintained. That such a life is impossible to live has not been refuted either logically or practically. To suggest that it is impossible based on the static analysis of *immediate tradeoffs*, many of which have been established with complete disregard for risk, is short sighted and ridiculous.

Reflected at the most basic level of life, this wider view suggests that we can obtain at least a subsistence world at an agreeable level of minimal, natural risk. The harmony we obtain in such a world is represented in the ancient notion of the endless continuum of nature. This balance is often represented by the imagery of a snake eating its own tail: The *Ouroboros*, or Greek for "tail eater", as represented in Figure 7.2.

The limitedness of our existence says that since we can't have everything, abundance is not (currently) a

Figure 7.2 The notion of continuity … a *Balance of Nature*

factor of our existence. This means that we, as humans (as do all living creatures), have to figure out a way of living either within our limits or how to expand them safely. As a result, scarcity should be replaced with the ideas of continuous renewal, and living within the bounds of safety. It is this notion of infinite balance that lies at the root of the management of existential risk, not some appeal to incommensurate tradeoffs based on the immediate scarcity of worldly goods. The costs of a risk-free world are the same as its benefits. There is no distinction. What is the cost of natural actions such as breathing, thinking, laughing? Physiologically, we may look at them as the expenditure in biological energy we take to do these things. Yet, these merely physiological expenditures do not justify, nor do they explain, life. We certainly cannot tell based on such expenditures why it is better to breath (i.e., live) than not. If we can't justify the physiological aspects of life on the basis of simple costs and benefits, we certainly cannot justify its spiritual basis on them either.

The constraint-based approach to decision-making maintains the balance of nature since the constraints define conditions that simply cannot be violated in order to maintain this balance. These conditions are set by both logical analysis and experimentation. This analysis is, in turn, based on a deeper understanding of how life fits together in the natural world. A multi-criteria evaluation can in this way avoid some of the incommensurables found in a purely market-based assessment of the value of survival. Tradeoffs are still important, but where they are inappropriate, the multi-criteria system challenges them. The multi-criteria approach to decision provides for a holistic view of value that can be made more consistent with a moral view of the importance of survival, in its many facets. And should these constraints offer a roadblock to further progress, they trigger the search for better, risk-free alternatives.

Continuity is related to the idea of *sustainability*, which states that long-term survivability is based on our matching resource inflows and outflows. It goes beyond the mere physical balance of resource matching, however, to address the deeper question of how we live, or how we should live. From the idea of a natural balance, the idea of a resource balance follows. Sustainability in this regard is just another way of presenting our minimum standard for life. The baseline for resource usage and renewal is set at this point. As with all risk exposures, we maintain a suitably low risk of resource exhaustion in our quest for progress. Natural harmony can only be achieved by reference to a wider system, and our conscious working to preserve this harmony through planning. It is not about manipulating the system, it's about trying to fit in with it. The infinite valuation we place on human existence arises *only* within the context of the wider natural system. There is no intrinsic value to a single life, or even a society, outside this systematic existence.

Achieving the balance of continuity defines the idea of value via identity. What we value *is* this balance, for it sustains us. Can this balance take us beyond subsistence? Why not – there is no universal law of nature that says that nature is stingy in this regard. Nor is there any indication that we have to trade threats to our continued existence for happiness. The challenge is once again finding out how to live within this balanced approach, as individuals and, perhaps more importantly, as a society. Our intellectual powers are better utilized by trying to identify this balanced course from the beginning, rather than trying to figure out a way to correct for imbalances later on.

In basing our approach to life on a continuous process of renewal, we incorporate the survival ethic into our basic system of values. This valuation process lets us live life in this world as if our existence *really* mattered. A willingness to trade this existence for some short-term gains, on the other hand, shows how little we care – both for our own lives and for the lives of others.

Further reading

On the consistent economic undervaluation of life in the "free market" process, see *Priceless: On Knowing the Price of Everything and the Value of Nothing* (The New Press, 2004), by Frank Ackerman and Lisa Heinzerling.

Defects in market systems that rely on the self-centered quest for profits with respect to the issues of ecological degradation and its associated risks have been consistently documented in the rise of *eco-socialism*. Eco-socialist critiques concentrate on the fundamental weaknesses of market systems to adequately admit social costs. See, for example, J. Kovel's *The Enemy of Nature: The End of Capitalism or the End of the World* (Zed Books, 2007) and *Eco-Socialism or Eco-Capitalism?: A Critical Analysis of Humanity's Fundamental Choices* (St. Martin's Press, 1999) by S. Sarkar. Early criticisms of the market system's fundamental inability to capture the full social costs of modern progress include K. Willam Kapp's *Social Costs of Private Enterprise* (Harvard University Press, 1950).

For an overview of MCDM, see Milan Zeleny's *Multiple Criteria Decision Making* (McGraw Hill, 1982). On MCDM in the assessment of technological and social risks, see *Social Multi-Criteria Evaluation for a Sustainable Economy* (Springer, 2008), by Giuseppe Munda. Dr. Munda extends the idea of multi-criteria decisions to the realm of imperfect, yet useful, knowledge (i.e., *fuzziness*) in his book *Multi-Criteria Evaluation in a Fuzzy Environment* (Physica Verlag, 1995).

How business managers handle high-stakes business risks is described in Zur Shapira's *Risk Taking: A Managerial Perspective* (Russell Sage Foundation, 1995). Evidence of the reliance of business organizations on state-sponsored precautionary financial options is also shown in *When All Else Fails: Government as the Ultimate Risk Manager* (Harvard University Press, 2004), by David A. Moss. Commercial insurance remains an important first line of precautionary financial defense for the business enterprise, as documented in *Principles of Risk Management and Insurance* (Addison-Wesley, 2007), by George Rejda.

The idea of a flow, or natural balance, of nature as a foundation for a new ecological economics is explored in Joan Martinez-Alier's book, *Ecological Economics* (Blackwell, 1987). Especially noteworthy is the author's discussion of the philosopher/scientist Otto Neurath's concept of social and economic planning based on the notion of non-monetary tradeoffs (values "in kind"). Neurath's own conceptions were presaged by the ideas of economic balance in the works of the natural philosophers Josef Popper-Lynkeus and Karl Ballod-Atlanticus.

8
Achieving a Viable Utopia

Technological dreams of a world of plenty – complete utilitarian satisfaction – can turn into nightmares when their achievement depends on incurring increased uncertainty about doom. Casting our existence in terms of these tradeoffs only acts to devalue it. What then of a workable utopia that includes safe progress as one of its goals? The two fundamental choices remain: We can do nothing, enjoy the fruits of the high life, and wish for the best (optimism), recognizing that this position may bring ultimate doom. Alternatively, we can take action to avoid catastrophe. Utopia, it would seem, depends on our ability to reconcile these two choices. Yet, given the persistence of risk dilemmas, is such a feat possible?

Part of the answer, as suggested above, lies in the way we value the respective choices. *Acting* on this valuation, in turn, depends on our ability to recognize a teleology, or sense of purpose, in our being. The idea of natural balance suggests that survival can be made consistent with a rational fatalism, if we are prepared to live within that balance. With regard to high-stakes risk, that means maintaining a natural risk level. Survival in a wider social context requires that individual differences and inconsistencies in valuation of our existence be smoothed over. To recognize this wider context, we need to act in a collective fashion.

   While increasing uncertainty over the existential risks we face might eventually tip the scales in favor of such concerted action, the associated social risk may mean that such a realization will only come too late. This means meaningful action toward a coordinated democracy must be achieved sooner than later. In the mean time, then, the potential for finding a "way out" is what gives us *hope* for the future.

8.1   Assessing our prospects

The various technical and moral issues in the management of high-stakes risks need to be looked at in concert if we are to set and achieve reasonable goals associated with survival. What we know, or might reasonably know, about making choices in the face of high-stakes risks can be summarized as follows (all arising from our intuitive notions about high-stakes risks):

1. The uncertainties we face about high-stakes risk, those that go beyond randomness and into the realm of the imperfectly known, are a crucial feature in dealing with high-stakes risk.
2. Under conditions of high-stakes existential risk, only the decision options of fatalism (do nothing, and hope for the best) and precaution (avoid danger) make sense. Criteria in between, including those that depend on the statistical notion of averaging, do not make sense. Under the *catastrophe problem*, in the long run, there may be no long run.
3. A fatalism that involves mere acquiescence to risk does not remove uncertainty and the resulting worry. It is an uneasy fatalism at best, and could in and of itself *promote* dangerous outcomes. Natural levels of

risk reduce both the likelihood of a very bad outcome *and our uncertainty about these likelihoods.*

4. Precaution becomes practical under the idea of a natural level of risk, where we work to not exceed background risk.

5. Once risks become entrenched, applying sensible precautions becomes a virtually insurmountable challenge. Avoiding risk while at the same time avoiding *risk dilemmas* ("doomed if we do, doomed if we don't") requires thoughtful *pre*-planning, at a coordinated, social level.

6. The idea of resource use as continuous (preserving the *balance of nature*) suggests that the value of a naturally risk-free life is to be sought in the way we live that life, rather than in terms of tradeoffs against material gains. Only in this way can we pay proper respect to *moral absolutes.*

In recognizing these preconditions for survival, we must also understand that the prevailing system of treating high-stakes risk remains primarily utilitarian, often articulated formally using economic cost/benefit analysis. The strict utilitarian argues that this valuation should be based on tradeoffs among competing objectives. By following this approach, however, we give up on our most basic values too easily. Even absolutes, such as the survival of the world, are made to seem negotiable. On the other hand, the moralist's position, based solely on a deontology of what we *ought* to do, regardless of outcomes or ends, is often based only on sentiments, perhaps themselves driven by some degree of self-interest. As we have argued early on, a proper deontology must contain at least *some* element of consequence, or consideration of what will ultimately happen. A tough balance arises because what happens may ultimately be out of our control. What elements of influence we may have in this destiny depend on understanding our responsibilities toward the wider, cosmic (if you will) universe we are part of. That means trying to work within the fundamental teleology, or purpose, of existence of this universe and our part in it. *Absolutes can not be abandoned, as they are dictated by these universal laws.* That much we do know – or should, through both experience and a deeper intuition. Uncertainty only affects our quest for how to live within these laws.

We have argued also that the methods for a more survivable world exist in the precautionary approach to risk, based on maintaining natural risk levels. However, as we have shown above, the technical approach and a moral commitment in high-stakes risk are an inseparable combination. Precaution won't work, and indeed, can't work, without the proper moral attitude. And neither can this combination work without our resolve to implement a suitable social and economic structure to achieve a naturally risk-free life. To the extent we are unwilling to carry out any portion of this agenda, then our societal and economic systems will *not* function properly as a whole.

An approach to existential risk management based on natural precaution can have a happy ending for both the soft-edged moralist and the hard-line utilitarian. By practicing a naturally risk-free existence, we reconcile precaution with fatalism, achieving the good life, with the promise of sufficient certainty that we may exist long enough to fully appreciate it. The optimism that results is then truly sustainable. In the process we gain not only physical survival, but also an existence worth maintaining.

The big unknown remains a practical one, *can we get there from here*? Is the reconciliation of fatalism and precaution achievable by any reasonable means at our disposal, given what we have to work with as human beings? In light of the prospects we have outlined above, we need to examine what practical changes to our institutions, not just ourselves, can help us get on the right path. That path is the one away from disaster, and the uncertainties it entails, and toward a better life for all.

8.2 "Starting over" is not an option

Given what appears to be a predisposition to create risk dilemmas any way we turn from our current position, some observers suggest that the only way out of these difficulties may be to *start over*. This is achieved by reducing society to its most basic form, or to what we have referred to as its *subsistence level* with respect to risk. The shape of safe progress could then be determined, unfettered, based on this new starting point. Practically, how viable is such an option? Convincing people to voluntarily return to past times is an incredibly hard sell. The notion of a wholesale surrender of current comforts is far fetched, given the fact that it is the very risk dilemmas we are trying to avoid that seem to hold us in the present state. A voluntary return therefore becomes a contradiction of reality. On the other hand, a "clean slate" may be forced on us, cataclysmically, as a potential outcome of our current inattention to the problems of accumulating high-stakes risk. A realizable clean slate may not be so remote, given the scenarios we currently face with respect to high-stakes risk. The idea is then that transition to such a clean start would put value into proper perspective. The worth of this perspective is formalized today in the economists idea of *contingent valuation*, that is, the idea that we can assess the value something by taking it away – what if you didn't have it, how much would you pay to get it back? Obviously, this is a question we can only ask ourselves hypothetically, based on any voluntary return to a more basic life. Once again, hypothetical concerns may not seem very convincing. On the other hand, the admonition that "we never miss what we have until it's gone" represents the most bitter irony when we consider what's "gone" is our existence.

Even if the human race somehow survives to live again after some cataclysmic event, what would we do different, or would we in fact do it all again the same way? We might place all the warnings about the possibility of risk and the right way to do high-stakes risk management in a time capsule, as a warning to the new generation. Would it do any good? There are, and have been, plenty of warnings up to now. Have they worked?

A rebirth through the pain of starting over is an overly romantic notion that entails crucial risks of its own. It promotes a nihilistic acquiescence that may in fact hasten our demise. And for what? The chance that the extremely complex combination of factors that can support some degree of human subsistence would reappear from this nothingness is absolutely tiny. Too tiny it would seem to base future hope on. The end may very well be *the end* and not a new beginning.

Perhaps the outcome of our current path need not be as drastic. Might not our previous experience with at least partial disasters, in a smaller context, dictate the proper stance, precautionary or fatalistic? The problem is that our reactions to serious, let us call them *sub-catastrophic*, events tend to be proportional to their impact. As examples from modern history, take our reactions to the two world wars, various natural disasters, the Great Depression, the terrorist attacks of 9/11 – all reactions, while significant, seem to have been roughly proportional to damage done. This suggests that a 10 percent impact would have a 10 percent response, a 20, 20 percent response, and so on. The full response therefore corresponds to a 100 percent, or near 100 catastrophe (i.e., actual or near extinction). So while the clean slate represents an opportunity to learn from our mistakes, it is one that we may not live to take advantage of.

We need not abandon the idea of a clean slate completely, however. We just need to recognize that to be useful, the clean slate does not have to become a reality. As a vision, or as a guide to the properties that some desired end state *should* have, it can become a valuable part of the backcasting process. In this way we may not actually have to "start over" to achieve the benefits that at least the image of that new start may convey.

8.3   The survival ethic as collective sense of purpose

Avoiding the clean slate requires a reasonable commitment to an ethics of survival. It is commitment to this ethic that reconciles precaution, through pre*action*, and fatalism. In doing so, we recognize that we must coordinate our existence with the wider spectrum of nature, in the process making safe progress synonymous with fate. Our purpose (or *telos*) is a fundamental component of our intuitions about life (as formalized in the philosophy of the ancient Stoics, and shared with Eastern philosophies such as Taoism). It is, quite simply, *to live in harmony with nature*. However, as these ancient philosophies also recognized, in order to reach this wider goal, we may have to subordinate selfish interests. What has to be overcome is a powerful self-centered drive to achieve immediate satisfactions at the expense of future troubles. We need a way to avoid the outcomes that come from this tempting of fate.

The problem boils down to one of the *context* of survival, and the perspective that this context entails. By context, we mean that level at which survival affects us. This context may be purely individual, from the level of the business enterprise, the community, society, or even from the standpoint of the wider ecology of the planet. To say that each entity looks at survival differently is to overstress the differences, however. Many similarities of purpose exist. A degree of self-interest, or self-preservation, is one of them. In and of themselves, these differences need not interfere with the goals in successively wider contexts. That is, there is no reason to think that all contexts work *deliberately* at cross-purposes. The very idea of unity of purpose in life suggests that they don't. Yet, less deliberately, self-interest may migrate to selfishness, and result in some pathological outcomes, at least from the standpoint of a coordinated nature that includes all.

The philosopher/scientist Garrett Hardin has reflected on how individual human choices can paradoxically affect survival in a parable he calls the *tragedy of the commons*. In his scenario, the farmers of a small community share a common grazing area. The individual farmer feels that it is in his or her best interest to graze as many cattle as he or she can on the common land, assuring maximum personal utility for himself or herself. However, if all farmers try to maximize individual outcomes in this way, the commons disappears, and all life the animals that graze there support would cease to exist. The problem need not be just about trying to incrementally improve your lot at the expense of others. The farmer may view the situation as genuinely life threatening and hence self-preservative. He or she may genuinely believe that less than maximum grazing may threaten their existence. The paradox enters, in that overgrazing will threaten his or her livelihood as well. As in the risk dilemmas, the individual may feel "doomed if they do, doomed if they don't".

Hardin suggests that the situation, from an individual standpoint, may be simply irresistible – a part of human nature. His proposed solution is a coordinative one, which he describes quite succinctly as "mutual coercion, mutually agreed upon". Key to the workability of such a solution is the idea that there can be some agreed sharing of the commons (i.e., the means of existence) that promotes survival for all. The farmer's view that he or she must maximize grazing to survive is therefore incorrect. They labor under a false assumption that could spell disaster for all. It is similar false assumptions that, we would argue, distort the value proposition inherent in all progress. We are led to believe, or lead ourselves to believe, that survival is too costly. The balance of nature view suggests that it is not. As in the case of the classical risk dilemma, preventing the commons tragedy necessitates *pre-planning*. The outcome is just too important to leave to individualized interests.

In his assessment for overcoming the commons tragedy, Hardin also rightly places little value on the idea that humans can become self-interestedly enlightened into the realization that altruism trumps selfishness. The deep-seated reasons against such behavior are many and varied, perhaps controversial. They speak to the deeper nature of humankind. It may suffice at this stage to simply point out that it is just a fact of life. Individualized appeals to action for the avoidance of the commons tragedy, as in the case of risk dilemmas, appear futile. The answer lies rather in a *collective* realization and actualization of our sense of purpose.

8.4   Recognizing the authority of nature

The inescapable conclusion then is that some sort of coordinated guidance or planning is needed to avoid such dilemmas, and the tragedy of human existence they entail. This means that *our sense of purpose must come from above, not from within*. Nature commands our survival, and our goal is to recognize that authority. Outside this system, human survival – either individual or societal – does not matter. In order to harmonize with this authority, and to plan accordingly, some sort of guidance is needed on a coordinated level. This recognition may itself require society, or at least some representative vanguard thereof, to push an agenda for a radical (i.e., fundamental) rethinking. Actions must be controlled, in the sense of overriding strong individual tendencies to seek what is of most selfish utility, resulting from our individual incapacity to see the wider picture. Note that this incapacity need not be a result of some inherent badness in human nature. It is rather that we cannot see the whole picture from our limited vantage point as individual members of a wider system (both human and natural). To the extent that evolution itself can be shaped in terms of the common interest, that is, if we would be able to somehow mold human nature via its institutions into beings that care for this wider nature *automatically*, then any collective planning or control mechanisms become no longer necessary. They eventually become part of human nature. The point for now is that this natural response is clearly not automatic, and that significant change, in us and our institutions, is required to make it happen.

In this view, planning helps us coordinate goals among contexts. Likewise, the goal of collective planning is not to enforce morals, but to preserve a sense of collective purpose from which the proper ethic of survival follows. Through this exercise we achieve greater freedom, not less. Nonetheless, the type of system envisioned here may be viewed as requiring the exercise of some degree of authority, especially to the extent that any required planning is centralized. However, we do so simply to maintain the necessary discipline to achieve common goals. The degree of authoritarian control we accept in this regard is only that demanded by a natural order, nothing more. That regimes with some degree of authoritarian conduct, even if sanctioned by a democracy, can turn despotic is a fact that can be easily gleaned from observing history. This same history, however, can give us valuable insights in maintaining the proper degree of democratic involvement. Nothing suggests that increased attention to planning at the collective level necessarily leads to an *undemocratic* totalitarianism, and the abrogation of personal freedom.

As we have noted in our preceding discussions of planning, questions of implementation detail, such as the proper locus of planning (either centralized or decentralized), need to be addressed in conjunction with the idea of achieving a sense of purpose. Implementation, however, should not be controlled by our ideological fears. Centralization need not mean diminution of personal freedom. Likewise, decentralization need not suggest a dilution of purpose, or a return to more liberal notions, such as the faith in so-called "free" markets to achieve collective goals. As previously noted, decentralized decisions make sense when the problems are sufficiently within their scope, and they can properly reflect local conditions. Whatever solution we choose, centralized or decentralized, it is dictated by the problems at hand, not some preconceived commitment to what a proper system of governance *should* look like.

In the end, the failure of liberalized ideas of freedom and democracy can itself *reduce* our freedom. Freedom to do *anything*, even if it harms other humans, or the non-human environment with which we coexist, stretches both the human code, and the idea of a unity of nature and our place in it. Arguably, this liberalism has legitimized a growing disregard for others and our environment, which is tempered now only by the increasing uncertainty we feel as our relationships within society, and to our natural environment, become more complex.

The notion of achieving coordinated goals through the actions of some benevolent autocracy has lost much of its attraction in today's world precisely because we all feel we must preserve our individuality. More often than not this means we seek to stake selfish claims to what is becoming more and more a materially oriented existence. In doing so, however, we unwittingly acquiesce to a far more insidious "higher power" – one that doles out material satisfaction at the cost of long-run survival. This power cloaks itself by giving lip service to democracy and freedom. At the same time, it promulgates a more subtle abuse of our freedom to choose. We have attempted to outline above how such powerful self-interests can drastically undermine freedom from existential risk. The alleged "freedom" of markets and the social laws that support such markets can be manipulated to create a more subtle form of tyranny, yet one just as binding as that of the worst despot. And every tyrant knows it is easier to rule a crowd that in some way believes their subjugation is merely a factor of their own self-interest.

8.5   Beyond the "tipping point"

All that remains then for implementation is a final impetus for fundamental change. We have excluded some sort of spontaneous moral or physical rebirth as romantic products of the moralists' vision. All such views do is aid and abet incremetalism, and acquiescence. We have also dismissed the standard ploy of catastrophists and other doomsayers that *the end is near*. What will move us into action is *not* the threat of global warming to the health and well-being of the *next* generation, or even that millions meet their demise *today* through war, terror, and other acts of physical violence, as well as hunger and disease resulting from social status. It will not be that the person next door has died of cancer, or perhaps one of our relatives has just succumbed to an occupational disease. It may not even be that we have some incurable environmentally induced illness *ourselves*. Rather, it is *not knowing* if the next minute, year, or decade entails our collective demise that will push us past the "tipping point" for action.

The concern then is not about what random ball we draw next from the urn that the circumstances of our world have mixed. Rather, it is the subtler challenge that the urn has in some way been "stacked", or may have turned distinctly non-random in some unknown way. Add to this the differentials in exposure to potential risks between class, race and level of wealth, and this uncertainty builds a further atmosphere of distrust, even loathing. The uncertainties in this way perpetuate themselves, the fog gets thicker, and this uncertainty itself pushes us to an untimely end. Survival is concrete, but uncertainty about survival is palpable as well. It drives our concerns, and ultimately our demand for a better way, right now. This uncertainty is not just a matter of subjective perception, but of reality itself. The fuzzy intervals around some best guess of the likelihood of disaster are *real*. In terms of increasing complexity, we can measure the degree to which these intervals, and hence our concerns about uncertainty, are expanding.

Uncertainty, of course, complicates our commitment to moral absolutes. Some everyday actions, such as operating a motor vehicle, may subject others to extreme harm or even death, despite a strong commitment to the moral absolute against taking the life of another. Sometimes, so-called crimes of passion occur, committed by those who otherwise maintain a belief in the primacy of moral behavior. Both physical and psychological uncertainties due to imperfect knowledge will likely always be with us. Yet, is there any reason to believe that existing uncertainties overwhelm our ability to maintain absolutes, thereby pushing us into some inevitable state of moral indeterminacy? In the analysis of risk, we capture these uncertainties in the notion of fuzzy, or imperfectly known, thresholds. While imperfect, these fuzzy thresholds permit us to maintain a strong level of commitment to "doing the right thing", even though the outcomes of our actions are not always perfectly predictable.

When dealing with growing uncertainties that follow from increasing complexity we need to cope with two effects. One is the direct effect that uncertainty obscures the growth of existential risks. The indirect, or secondary, effect is that growing uncertainty causes a psychological reaction which may ultimately promote very strong (i.e., *revolutionary*) reactions. Today's socio-technological systems are volatile, as a direct result of their complexity. Just like highly combustible physical substances, all it takes is one spark to ignite a massive explosion. Growing uncertainty may create the spark that sets our social system into upheaval.

How do we cope with such massive upsets? Most modern democratic societies have some provisions for sovereign *emergency powers*. In situations of pending societal disintegration or chaos, brought on by man-made perils such as war, or the threat of war, or natural ones such as natural disasters, concerted control and planning is looked to for relief. In such times, we recognize the need for a strong coordinated effort to fight some human or natural foe. Sometimes such efforts of last resort are successful, sometimes not. To the extent they are not, there is little hope of starting over from nothing. Are we approaching a *state of emergency* with respect to the risks we face? If so, then crisis planning may or may not help avert disaster. We need to plan ahead, *before* it is too late.

8.6   On hope and the future

The unknown fuels a cycle of despair. The presence of risk dilemmas, regardless of how hard special interests may try to disguise them as utilitarian cost/benefit tradeoffs or whatever, leads to a feeling that there may be no way out. This leads to risk acquiescence – the acceptance of risk under the feeling that we have no choice. Mere acquiescence is not satisfying, and leads to increasing uncertainty, and ultimately despair in finding a reasonable solution.

We have suggested that a suitable planning structure, based on natural risk levels, can help break this cycle. A socio-economic system that helps assure survival will be one that can recognize and implement a commitment to moral absolutes. Following this course, it can also reduce uncertainty about survival. Can such a system be achieved, practically? Again, coordinated implementation of plans may itself be the most natural response to risk in a complex society. Our decision to *let* ourselves follow this course, however, will require some soul searching and ultimately the ability to properly recognize a sense of purpose. That we will achieve all these, and reasonably assure our survival in the process, cannot be determined ahead of time, nor will the outcomes become immediately apparent. The wider framework in which the quest for survival operates, therefore, requires *hope* for the future. The basis of this hope is not a blind optimism in some technological solution to our problems, or even the ability to sense some deeper moral purpose in it all. Rather it will require a reasoned idea of what we, and the world, can become. Uncertainty, of course, makes any such goals in at least some sense fantastic, perhaps just a mere *image* of what we might consider the "good life". The dream becomes unabashedly utopian. The point is that such utopias are necessary, nonetheless, to promote hope.

Utopias may be either *abstract* or *concrete*. Both types have a use in instilling hope. The abstract utopia is based on an image of how things may be, in line with our purpose in life. The abstract utopia is always in a state of becoming, or what philosopher Ernst Block called the "not yet". It gives us the vision needed to kindle our desire to achieve more than we have, to go beyond mere acquiescence. The concrete utopia is one of attainment. Concrete utopias *are* the achievement, at least to some palpable degree, of our dreams. The concrete utopia proves that these dreams can be made a reality. To achieve concrete utopia we need the tools and techniques to do so. Here, we suggest that democratic planning can make utopia a reality. Exploration (i.e., backcasting) from hopes and goals leads to concrete action toward a safer future and, at the same time, reinforces our sense of purpose. As it turns out survival is a very primitive need which in today's world can only be satisfied by more complex means.

To be sure, a strong *anti-utopian* camp exists today. Some see the idea of utopia based on its literal translation as "nowhere". It is an unachievable fiction, whose promulgation does nothing but offer only *false* hope. Anti-utopians are not united in their underlying philosophy, however. Some simply see utopia as a threat to special interests. They resist the notion of a selfless utopia based on its threat to these selfish interests. Market systems are often posed as being realistic, as opposed to being "merely" utopian, in the very sense that they offer concrete utilitarian solutions to the problems we face. This view is strongly influenced by the philosophy of *what is, is what ought to be*, or in other words, the view we live in the best possible world (as directed either by God, self-interest, or some other power). As we have suggested above, the best possible world view is usually offered as simply an apology for maintaining the status quo.

On the other hand, there are those that view the course of the world as clearly *dystopian*, or as having an inevitable "bad ending". We further subdivide these thinkers as *romanticists* and *nihilists*. The romanticist believes in the notion of destruction followed by rebirth. Perhaps we might better classify these types as *born again utopians* rather than as pure anti-utopians, or dystopians. Renewal occurs until we achieve long-run success – a sort of iterative process that may span eons. The nihilist, on the other hand, subscribes to the more dire conclusion that anti-utopia, or dystopia, *is* our fate – with the ultimate outcome being that humans were simply not meant to survive.

Yet others identify utopianism with its purely technological strain. The result sets us up for a paradoxical utopia of abundance that comes only at the expense of our ultimate demise (hence, the *paradox of progress*). A true utopia cannot be built on such logical inconsistencies, regardless of how attractive they may appear in the short run.

A genuine utopianism can only be based on seeking a *natural* order. We need to work toward discovering this natural state and functioning within it, rather than trying to supplant nature using science and technology. To be sure, there may be technological and scientific miracles that have contributed and will continue to contribute to progress toward utopia. Collective planning assures that such progress, however, stays on the right path. Planning against a technological dystopia is our best hope of preventing one.

Even though survival seems to be the *sine qua non* of utopian visions, to believe that humanity will survive forever is not a tenable proposition. We have to concede that purely on the basis of realism, and logical extrapolation from past experience. We may not know everything about our world, but even our most basic evolutionary arguments suggest that nothing on this earth survives forever, and from what we can reasonably infer from the history of our universe, not even the earth itself can survive through eternity. However, the very notion of survival implies, once again, working within the wider system (i.e., the wider cosmos), in accordance to our perceived *telos*, or purpose. We all know that as individuals we must die sometime. That does not mean that we should live life with careless abandon in the mean time.

Just as the Stoic philosophers quite honestly observed early on in human history, everything reduces to fate. It is fate therefore that shapes what we should value, and ultimately what we describe as the ethic of survival. We try to assess the potentials logically, applying whatever hazy empirical guidance we can muster. Utopia-building then must be in tune with the notion of fate, which in turn is simply a matter of preserving natural order. Perverse utopian visions, which ultimately have bad endings for all of us, are created when we try to work against the forces of nature. Through planning for a naturally risk-free existence we are suggesting an alternative pathway of progress that leads toward a *viable* utopia. And that is all we need to have hope. Hope, it would seem, is another innate quality of our species, possibly driving the need for survival itself. For without hope, we are already doomed.

Further reading

Garrett Hardin has written extensively on what we call the *contextual* effects of risk and survival. Hardin published his most widely read version of the "Tragedy of the Commons" in the periodical *Science*, December 13, 1968. Hardin's exposition of the implications of the tragedy for modern life and the risks it entails appeared in his book *Exploring New Ethics for Survival* (Viking Press, 1972), complete with a reprint of the original article.

The potential defects of our increasingly liberalized democracies to promote wider social goals were noted as early on de Tocqueville's post-American revolution *Democracy in America* (Viking Penguin, 2003), originally published in 1835. The inter-world war period of the early twentieth-century spawned further probing into democratic systems for social change, and the possibility of planned social systems, in the works of sociologist Karl Mannheim, most notably in *Man and Society in the Age of Reconstruction* (Harcourt, Brace, 1940) and *Freedom, Power and Democratic Planning* (Oxford, 1950). The tradition of a notion of control under democracy continued with Herbert Marcuse, *One Dimensional Man: Studies in the Ideology of Advanced Industrial Society* (Beacon Press, 1964), appearing roughly coincidentally with the rise of the ecological consciousness in the 1960s. From the time of Marcuse and Commoner's work (cited above) during this period, risk awareness (especially from an ecological perspective) and a search for the true meaning of freedom in the modern age have been intertwined.

For more on the idea of centralized control in cases of a national (or world) emergency, as it pertains to the government of the United States of America, see *National Emergency Powers*, a report compiled by the *Congressional Research Service*, and issued August 30, 2007. The study details numerous exercise of this power in the United States, in times of stress from natural events and geo-political events which threatened our national security. That such actions are often just a prelude to collapse can be gleaned from studies of societal decay, such as Joseph Tainter's *Collapse of Complex Societies* (Cambridge University Press, 1990).

The philosopher Ernst Block traces the intertwined history of utopian ideas and their relevance to the idea of hope in his work *The Principle of Hope* (MIT Press, 1986), a translation of his three-volume work in German, *Das Prinzip Hoffnung*, published in 1954. The *cycle of despair* that uncertainty creates can be related to the collapse of utopian ideals, and the lack of hope. That upheaval may ensue to regain hope in such situations is argued in Melvin Lasky's *Utopia and Revolution* (University of Chicago Press, 1976).

On modern trends in anti-utopian thought, see Krishan Kumar's *Utopia and Anti-Utopia in Modern Times* (Blackwell, 1987). Many literary works are cited as warnings against "utopias gone bad", including George Orwell's classic, *1984*, first published in 1946. Often such works are not anti-utopian per se, but are rather subtly suggestive of pitfalls to watch for. With regard to Orwell's dystopian writings, see *The Orwell Conundrum: A Cry of Despair, or Faith in the Spirit of Man?* (McGill University Press, 1992), by Erika Gottlieb. More often than not, modern literature, film, and television (including Orwell's) offer dystopian views in criticism of false *technological* utopias, many of them emphasizing the paradox that the risks of unbridled technological progress entail.

For current views on utopia and the future of human existence, see *Viable Utopian Ideas: Shaping a Better World* (M. E. Sharpe, 2003), edited by Arthur B. Shostak. See also *Utopia and the Millennium* (Reaktion Books, 1997), a series of contributions edited by Krishan Kumar and Stephan Bann.

Appendix A
The Intuitive Principles of Risk

1. In general, *risk* is a word used to describe adverse consequences that occur by chance. Depending on its probability/consequence characteristics, a risk can be a mere nuisance, a source of unwelcome (and possibly quite costly) variability, or a danger to our existence. We need to carefully delineate these properties when dealing with risk.
2. Risk is a physical property of the world, not some abstract mathematical concept. To understand risk, we need to understand its physical properties. Mathematical analysis is not enough. To be useable, the analysis must be concrete, not abstract.
3. Statistical risks manifest themselves over a relatively observable time frame, and are amenable to management via cost/benefit calculations based on averages, or expected values. Catastrophic risks are rare, but their consequences are enormous. We don't get a "second chance". They cannot be treated statistically since in the long run, there is no long run (the *Catastrophe Problem*).
4. In dealing with high-stakes risks, uncertainties due to knowledge imperfection enter. The probabilities of rare, complex events simply cannot be known with any degree of precision. We need to consider uncertainty due to knowledge imperfection, in addition to randomness, when making decisions about these risks.
5. The crucial first step in the high-stakes decision process is recognizing the possibility of serious adverse consequences, that is, those exposures that may fall into the *danger zone*. We need to be especially cautious with exposures that may increase the natural, or background, level of risk.

6. When risks are catastrophic, only two decision criteria make sense: Precautionary avoidance or fatalistic acceptance ("if it happens, it happens"). There is no in-between. Reconciling the two is the key function of risk management.
7. Precautionary avoidance of catastrophic risks can be expensive. By avoiding some risky activities, we may also forgo critical benefits. The result is *Risk Dilemmas*: We are doomed if we do, doomed if we don't. Post-fact risk management – managing catastrophic risks only after they become entrenched – exacerbates the dilemma. The careful analysis of alternatives, early on in the process of planning for progress (i.e., *preaction*), can help eliminate these dilemmas.
8. Those affected by high-stakes risks must ultimately make the decisions about their treatment. To prevent against the threat of being misled, intentionally or unintentionally, decision-makers need to *cultivate their innate intuitions about risk*.

Appendix B
A Glossary of Key Concepts

Absolutes (moral) – In moral philosophy, those things which cannot be compromised. The existence of absolutes shows respect for the existence of certain inviolable laws in the wider **cosmos**. Absolutes both define, and are defined by, our sense of purpose, or **teleology**. The existence of absolutes in this sense reflects our *strength of purpose*. See also Kant's **categorical imperative**.

Acceptable risk criterion – A risk level that while not strictly zero is low enough to be deemed rationally acceptable. **Natural risk levels** often provide a reasonable risk acceptance criterion based on the long observed streak of evolutionary survival they promote. Not to be confused with mere **acquiescence**, due to **desensitization**, force, or trickery.

Acquiescence (to risk) – The acceptance of risk with no effort to change either it or ourselves. Implies acceptance of risk levels considerably above those considered natural.

Alternatives assessment – In high-stakes risk management, the identification, and implementation, of safe (i.e., naturally risk-free) pathways to progress. Contrast to the **identify–assess–treat (I-A-T) model**, **feedback**, and **statistical risk** methods in general. Alternatives assessment helps prevent risk dilemmas by addressing potential high-stakes risk *before* they become entrenched.

Authoritarian(ism) – The precept that social control is best established "from above", through some directive, coordinating power. While most often associated today with despotic excess, history views authoritarian regimes, including benevolent autocracies of the past (both religious and secular), in a better light.

Authority of nature – The idea that recognizing the power of nature holds the best hope of human survival, or at least achieving our fate (whatever that may be) in the most agreeable fashion.

Average – The long-run outcome of a random series. See also **probability**.

Avoidance – Managing high-stakes risks by staying away from exposures to them. See also **precaution**.

Backcasting – A heuristic scenario-based technique of planning that works "backward" from desired goals to possible alternative pathways to achieve these goals. In high-stakes risk, backcasting is used to identify alternatives for safe paths toward progress. The process is heuristic, in that it attempts to discover new and novel ways to achieve hard safety goals (i.e., **naturally risk-free living**). See also **alternatives assessment**.

"Bait-and-switch" – A sales fraud that works by enticing the consumer with the promise of a remarkable "deal" (the bait), only to switch to a much less attractive offer once the customer arrives at the store. In the meantime, the customer has incurred considerable **sunk cost**, which includes their travel time and expense. In which case, the customer seems to have little choice but to take the considerably worse deal, or incur the sunk cost for nothing. In high-stakes risk, the idea of "no progress without risk" acts as a bait-and-switch, enticing the unwary into an attractive future that subsequently sours in the face of mounting uncertainties about our existence. By abandoning the sunk cost of the related infrastructure and our reliance on it at this point means we are "doomed if we do, doomed if we don't". We are in this way essentially "tricked" into potentially irresolvable risk dilemmas.

Balance of nature – The idea that fundamental nature is about achieving an equality, and not a tradeoff, per se, between resources and needs. Risk arises when we disturb this balance. The eternal renewal this idea entails is represented in ancient symbols of a snake eating its own tail (the **Ouroboros**, or Greek for "tail eater").

Best possible world – The idea that the world we live in is the best possible world. Promotes risk acquiescence.

Catastrophe – Large-scale damage that irreparably, perhaps fatally, harms the entity subject. Large-scale impacts are irreversible, we don't get a second chance. See (the) **catastrophe problem**.

(The) Catastrophe problem – The challenge of high-stakes risks lies in their terminal nature: In the long run, there may be no long run. As a result, statistical methods do not apply.

Categorical imperative – The dictum, associated with the eighteenth-century philosopher Immanuel Kant, that states that categorical moral maxims (what we *ought* to do) are only those that can at the same time be realized as universal laws. See **absolutes**.

Centralized (or **Central**) **planning** – Planning at some higher level, usually at the highest levels of the economy, or society in general. Most often associated with state (national) or government planning.

Chance – See **randomness**.

Clean-slate option – The idea of starting over once ruin occurs (assuming, of course, there is anyone, or anything, left to do so).

Co-fated events – The Stoic belief that certain events, though ultimately fated, coincided with others without which they would not be. For example, seeing a doctor when you have an illness is co-fated with getting better. The idea of co-fated events counteracts the idea that fatalism equates to idleness, or mere acquiescence to all around us.

Consequentialism – The general line of moral thought which suggests our choices be based solely on their outcomes, or consequences. See **utilitarianism**.

Constraints – In formal decision processes, some property that cannot be exceeded (e.g., **natural risk levels**).

Continuity – The purpose of life is represented by an infinite continuity of resources – the "stuff" of life. This continuity is often represented in the spiritual realm as a snake eating its own tail. This view of life is in distinct contrast to the idea of scarcity and tradeoffs that drives modern economic thought. See **balance of nature**.

Control – Making sure that plans are executed as made. See also **planning**. Like planning, the idea of control is part of the natural process.

Cosmos – A general term for the wider nature of things, that is, those effects both observable and unobservable. Goes beyond physical nature to include the (as yet) unobservable, or not completely definable.

Cost/benefit analysis – The analysis of decisions based on a comparison of resources (costs) and benefits (in its utilitarian version, human happiness, or pleasure). Actions should be taken only if they provide net pleasure over resources or effort expended. In some cases, may be extended to absolutes via considerations of infinite utility (or disutility). In high-stakes risk management, improperly valued costs and benefits can be used to obscure true risks, and promote acquiescence. See also **statistical risk**.

Cybernetics – The theory of planning and control of complex, dynamic systems.

Danger – See **catastrophe**.

Danger zone – That (fuzzy) level of risk at which impacts are catastrophic and the probability of impact is at least possible.

Decentralized planning – Coordinated planning at a more fragmented, or communal, level. Although decentralized planning may be more responsive to the need of the individual, it usually requires at least some sort of centralized oversight, especially for naturally large-scale or pervasive societal and economic issues, like risk. Contrast **centralized** (or **central**) **planning**.

Deep ecology – An ecological approach to physical nature that values non-human survival as much as human survival.

Democracy – The idea that decisions that concern a society are best made by the members of that society, acting in some concerted fashion. Democratic ideals must be reconciled with the potentials for the **Tragedy of the Commons** and other paradoxes of self-interested behavior. Democracy based on majority rule may not always be consistent with **freedom**.

Deontology – A moral philosophy which dictates actions we *ought* to take, with regard to ourselves, others, and the natural world. Our deontology is usually based on the idea of **absolutes**, absolute commitments, without regard to expected outcomes. While deontology is often contrasted with **consequentialism**, it is likely that any realistic deontology cannot ignore outcomes entirely. Deontology and consequences may in fact be united by our achieving a suitable sense of purpose, or **teleology**.

Desensitization – Acquiescence to high-stakes risk based on repeated exposures that dull the sense that such risk levels may be too high.

Disutility – The negative "want satisfying power" or loss (monetary, physical, or psychological) associated with some choice. Contrast **utility**.

Dystopia – Envisions a world where our worst fears are coming true. The "opposite" of **utopia**.

Emergence – See **emergent properties**.

(The) Environment – See **physical nature**.

Ethics – See **moral philosophy**.

Existence – See **survival**.

Exploratory modeling – A method of dealing with complex system models under uncertainty by identifying multiple plausible candidates, rather than a single precise model. This allows for increased flexibility in dealing with such models. See also **backcasting**.

Externalities – General name for costs that may not be captured in the standard economic methods of determining cost, and hence remain *external* to the process. Economic theory deals with externalities by trying to make them part of the cost equation, that is, internalizing them, once they become known. Market systems based on the notion of profit maximization are naturally incentivized to discount such costs, thereby increasing direct profits.

Fail safe – A property of systems in which should some component of the system cease to function, that discontinuity in itself does not imperil the entire system.

Fatalism – Generally, the doctrine that all things happen as they will. With regard to high-stakes decision, the choice of "doing nothing", so that everything that will be, will be. A wider fatalism encompasses the idea of responsibility, where our character determines, or at least does not interfere with, our fate. A narrow fatalism confuses the wider definition with mere acquiescence, or acceptance, without regard for any deeper responsibilities. A reasoned fatalism was central to the influential philosophy of the **Stoics**.

Fate – According to the Stoic philosopher Chrysippus (born 280 BC), fate is

> a certain natural arrangement of the universe, with things following upon other things and being involved with other things from eternity, such a weaving being inexorable.

Fate is consistent with **optimism** about our survival, but only if we live a life that is consistent with natural risk levels.

Feedback – The ability to control a system based on comparing actual performance with goal performance. Feedback is a short-run control mechanism that can easily lead to ineffective outcomes if applied to long-run trends.

Feedforward – Control of a system based on some model of the system itself. Feedforward is accomplished by applying suitable control signals to the models, so that desired changes can be achieved before something "goes wrong". See also **backcasting**.

Freedom – The absence of coercion or constraint in the ability to achieve a balance with nature. Freedom from risk requires that no individual be subject to risks beyond their will. The quest for freedom, therefore, must always be observed within the context of our **moral philosophy**.

Free market – See **market**.

Frequency interpretation (of probability) – An interpretation of probability as the outcome of a long-run series of events. See **average**.

Fuzziness – A way of expressing uncertainties due to knowledge imperfection, based on intervals of possibility graded by level of confidence.

Fuzzy – See **fuzziness**.

High-stakes risk – Large impact risks subject to the *catastrophe problem*. High-stakes risk cannot be treated with *statistical* methods. Synonyms: **catastrophe, danger.**

Hope, The principle of – The idea that **utopia** may someday become a reality.

Identify–assess–treat (I-A-T) model – A model for the treatment of statistical risk, based on identifying threats, assessing their impacts, and treating them so as to reduce or eliminate the risk. Effective application of the I-A-T model requires feedback of model performance, and hence can only be used for **statistical**, short-term, risks.

Incremental approach – Treating high-stakes risk piecemeal, or one at a time. Usually based on the idea that we can't control all high-stakes risks, thereby increasing rather than reducing the potential for risk dilemmas.

Incrementalism – See **incremental approach.**

Indeterminancy – A completely chaotic world in which no regularities are discernable, that is, complete randomness.

Infinite disutility – The idea that some risks carry with them the possibility of infinite "badness", or **disutility**. Risks to human survival and the nature that supports survival are often considered infinite, or near infinite. See **absolutes.**

Instrumental analysis – A precursor of **backcasting** suggested by economist Adolph Lowe, instrumental analysis involves solving problems by working backward to possible solutions, or *instruments*, based on the specification of goals.

Interval (of uncertainty) – Expression of uncertainty due to knowledge imperfection based on determining a simple interval which could possibly contain the exact definition, or measurement, of the concept under examination. See also **fuzziness.**

Intuition – The experiential knowledge that humankind has accumulated over time that is difficult to articulate precisely, yet provides a crucial guide to life.

Knowledge imperfection – A form of uncertainty that results from imperfections in our knowledge, or inability to identify a concept with precision. Uncertainty due to knowledge imperfection is distinct from randomness, though the two can coexist (e.g., in draws from an urn or bowl whose contents are not well specified, and subject to change). See also **fuzziness, interval (of uncertainty).**

Likelihood – See **probability.**

Market – A formalized means of exchange, in which the transactions of individuals themselves determine economic outcomes. Market valuations are driven by self-interest and measured in purely utilitarian terms. Also referred to as the *free market,* due to the (alleged) absence of constraints.

Minimax – A principle of decision which suggests that we make choices under extreme uncertainty so as to minimize the maximum loss, or disutility, regardless of likelihoods.

Mixed economy – An economy that contains elements of both **markets** and **planning**.

Moral philosophy – The theory of rights and duties of humans to themselves, other humans, and the wider natural environment.

Morals – See **moral philosophy.**

Multi-criteria decision-making (MCDM) – The use of criteria besides purely monetary ones in making complex risk decisions. May include the use of *constraints* to represent *absolutes*.

"Mutual coercion, mutually agreed upon" – A phrase coined by the philosopher/scientist Garrett Hardin that represents a "way out" of social risk dilemmas (as expressed in his **Tragedy of the Commons**). It implies that tough social issues may need to be tackled from the standpoint of some collective plan, with commensurate controls, in which the individuals controlled may have to give up some level of individual freedom to achieve collective success (i.e., *freedom is the recognition of necessity*).

Natural order – See **nature**.

Natural risk – Risk in the physical world just consistent with human subsistence. See **naturally risk free**.

Naturally risk free – Based on achieving risk levels that while not strictly zero, do not add substantially to the background level of risk appearing in the *physical* natural world. Based on some **subsistence level** of human existence, in which humans are just barely able to survive. The assumption is that this very basic level of risk has supported human life on this planet for thousands of years.

Nature – All physical nature, plus the wider scope of the system of existence that may go beyond the physical (or at least the physical as we know, and perhaps ever can know it). See **cosmos**.

Optimism – The psychological state of hoping for a positive outcome, despite incurring the potential of disaster through unbridled progress. By failing to take active precautions, we are left only with this optimism as our balance against extinction.

Ouroboros (**"tail eater"**) – Mystic symbol depicting a snake eating its own tail. The symbolism is meant to represent constant renewal, eternity, and the **balance of nature**. The idea lies beneath modern concept of **sustainability**.

(The) Paradox of progress – The idea that we can only achieve utopia under the threat of immanent destruction.

Physical nature – The properties of the tangible natural world around us, including humans, animals, plants, and the earth itself.

Planning – Developing a formal course of action with regard to some outcome(s). Planning for survival is part of our natural existence, not some forced extension of it.

Preaction – Determining (naturally) risk-free alternatives early on in the process of **planning** for **progress**.

Precaution – The avoidance of catastrophic outcomes. See **minimax**.

Precautionary principle – A principle of practical decisions under high-stakes risks with uncertainty due to knowledge imperfections, which suggests that we should avoid possible high-stakes outcomes, even though their probabilities are only vaguely known. Precaution is embodied in the simple principle "better safe than sorry".

Probability – A measure of uncertainty due to **randomness**. The occurrence of some event cannot be specified with certainty ("for sure"), but is only revealed as a tendency that makes itself known through repeated observations over time. Under the frequency definition, the probability that some event x will occur, $P(x)$, can be expressed using the simple ratio,

$$P(x) = \frac{\text{Number of outcomes in which x occurs}}{\text{Total number of outcomes}}$$

See also **randomness, propensity interpretation**.

Progress – The ability of humans to further satisfaction of their wants and desires. Safe progress is judged by how far we can get beyond the **subsistence level**, and maintain consistency with natural risk levels.

Propensity interpretation (of probability) – An interpretation of **probability** in terms of the physical tendencies of potential outcomes. The propensity view allows interpretation of probabilities applied to single event, rather than a series of events.

Purpose (sense of) – See **teleology**.

Radical rethinking – A reappraisal of set thought patterns, in light of a commitment to fundamental (i.e., basic) change, in both our ideas and actions.

Random – See **randomness**.

Randomness – A form of uncertainty that arises from our not being able to specify the initial conditions that determine some outcome exactly, thereby introducing variability. This variability can manifest itself as a regularity over time, in terms of an event's **probability**.

Regulation (of risk) – Risk control based on the idea of altering currently existing markets. Regulation on this basis is subject to "capture" or influence by powerful entities which have some degree of control over these markets (most often, the regulated entities themselves). Regulation is an **incremental approach** to high-stakes risk.

Regulative control – The process of control that changes system variables to achieve set goals. Works within the natural system, not outside (like **regulation**). In the human system, regulative control includes breathing, the heartbeat, and control of motor functions. See **cybernetics**.

Responsibility – The idea that we need to shape our character to live in proper harmony with nature, and by failing to do so, we make life more difficult for ourselves and others, in terms of "fitting in" with our deeper purpose (whatever that purpose may ultimately be).

Risk – Negative impacts that occur with some degree of **probability** (i.e., they are not certain).

Risk accumulation (fuzzy) – The idea that the accumulation of individual risks toward catastrophe can only be very imperfectly specified (i.e., is subject to considerable uncertainty due to knowledge imperfection). This interpretation suggests that we must be very cautious in adding possible catastrophic risks when their properties are at least to some extent unknown.

Risk dilemma – Situations that arise when, under application of precaution (minimax), any choice of action (including inaction) results in equally catastrophic outcomes. We become, in a sense, "doomed if we do, doomed if we don't". The only way out is *preaction*.

Risk management – The elimination of worry about the outcomes of **random** events. Can only be achieved by reconciling fatalism (do nothing, and don't worry about it) and precaution (avoid risk). This, in turn, can only be achieved by making precaution a natural (i.e., naturally *regulative*) reaction to our world. This, can only be achieved through maintaining the **balance of nature**.

Robustness – A property of planning for risk that allows options for safe progress that protect against the various contingencies that may arise. Robustness of plans is needed to counteract *uncertainty*.

Safety – Freedom from (unnatural) risk. See **natural risk level**.

Safety cushion – That level of risk between low natural risk levels and observable statistical risk. Uncertainties about risk measurement suggest that by accepting risk within this region we remove a level of protection against risks that may have been somehow underestimated.

Scarcity – Modern economics is pervaded with an idea of scarcity of resources, against which we must make tradeoffs to survive. Economics often manipulates decisions so that survival can be made to look like a tradeoff in the face of this scarcity. This view is short sighted, with the idea of continuity being a more natural model of life in harmony with the wider cosmos. Suggests the boundaries of the **danger zone** are only very imperfectly known.

Second-order (meta) cybernetics – A study of cybernetic control systems based on the idea that these control systems themselves operate within a wider teleology that must be considered for controls to be ultimately effective in achieving some degree of natural order (and hence natural safety goals).

Self-interest – The selfish seeking of personal, or closed communal (group), goals, to the exclusion of those interests of the wider human community and the environment.

Socio-technological risk – The idea that high-stakes technical risks influence, and indeed help promulgate, high-stakes social risks.

Statistics – The study of physical manifestations of probability, that is, in terms of actual observed outcomes.

Statistical risk – Risk subject to identification over some reasonable period of observation.

Stoics – An early philosophy that recognized that human purpose lies within the deeper purpose of the universe around us, much of which we cannot know and may never be able to understand fully. At the center of Stoic philosophy is the notion of fate, which the Stoics believed to be synonymous with this complex, yet ordered, universe. Despite their belief that our lives were determined by this cosmic order, most Stoics believed that fate was compatible with personal responsibility. Living within this order, or balance of nature, was to live the "good life". The degree of anyone's satisfaction in life, and indeed survival, was dependent on achieving a character consistent with this natural order.

Subsistence level (of risk) – That level of risk at which human beings are barely able to survive. True progress is measured by how far we can get beyond this subsistence level *safely*.

Sunk cost – A cost once incurred that becomes irretrievable. **Risk dilemmas** occur as sunk costs of a risky infrastructure built without our knowledge, only to present insurmountable obstacles to returning to a naturally risk-free level of existence.

Supply and demand – The primary method of expressing value-based decisions on production and consumption in the market economy. Assumes all values can be measured in relative terms (i.e., as tradeoffs).

Survival – Most basically, continued existence. A wider definition accommodates the idea that under certain regimes, psychological stress or otherwise diminished capacity (i.e., below accepted subsistence levels) may not be worth mere physical existence.

Survival ethic – **Moral philosophy** applied to **survival**.

Sustainability – The idea of survival is promulgated by matching resource usage with resource renewal. See **balance of nature**.

Taoism – Eastern philosophy that recognizes that a proper view of life must take into consideration the wider natural universe, and that our values are driven by finding our place in that universe. Compare **Stoics**.

Teleology – A philosophy based on determining the goals, or purpose of life. It is likely that this purpose can never be completely discovered by us, and as a result, **absolutes** may need to coexist with **utilitarian** values. A properly constructed teleology, therefore, can accommodate both **deontology** and **consequentialism**.

Telos – Purpose. See **teleology**.

Tipping point – That point at which uncertainty about existential risks becomes unbearable, resulting in revolt, chaos, and quite possibly, ensuing destruction.

Tolerable risk – A regulatory notion that suggests some risks above natural levels may be at least temporarily acceptable, until we find lower cost methods of reducing them. A variant of **cost/benefit analysis**.

Tradeoffs – The idea that pervades conventional economics is that our goals, including survival, are only achieved by trading off other interests, due to a fundamental scarcity of resources. The idea of tradeoffs is itself based on a narrow view of existence, which promotes special interest by manipulating human values in favor of short-run, utilitarian goals. Market systems (and as a result, market-based regulations) can only deal with such short-sighted tradeoffs. Contrast the **balance of nature**.

(The) Tragedy of the Commons – A dilemma that arises from the fact humans will always be inclined to acting in a short-term, self-interested manner, eschewing the sacrifices that are necessary to achieve precaution, thereby making risk dilemmas inevitable. Fundamentally, the tragedy assumes precaution can never be reconciled with fatalism, and that fatalism must always carry with it the negative stigma of acquiescence. This makes any form of risk management ineffective, and hence we are always subject to the worry that existential risks entail. In the end, the **paradox of progress** is inescapable.

Uncertainty – The inability to determine outcomes exactly. Major categories include **randomness** and **knowledge imperfection**. Growing uncertainty about the risks associated with progress may be the greatest threat to our mental and physical survival.

Urn model (of probability) – A way of visualizing the frequency interpretation of **probability** as physical draws of colored balls from a well-mixed urn, or bowl. In a sense, all decisions involving chance are like drawing from an urn of colored balls.

Utility – Want-satisfying power of some choice. Contrast **disutility**.

Utilitarian – A notion related to **consequentialism** that suggests all choices be made so as to maximize human satisfaction, or pleasure. Assumes consequences can always be measured, and hence traded, in relative terms. Absolutes suggest infinite **utility** (or alternatively, infinite **disutility**).

Utopia – An ideal world, in which the harmony of outcomes, both human and natural, is expressed as a balance between the two. Utopias, in a concrete sense, can act as a goal, and therefore a basis for a more comprehensive **backcasting** exercise which seeks to establish reasonable means of achieving this ideal state. Viable utopias must be distinguished from those built on false hopes based on the promise of technological progress, which when not properly monitored only leads to the **paradox of progress**.

Value – In **moral philosophy**, a measure of the worth or desirability of some thing or action. Value is ultimately determined by our teleology, or purpose in life. Viewing life as a **balance of nature**, what is of highest value, then, is what harmonizes our life to this wider **cosmos**, or natural purpose. This introduces the idea of **absolutes** to the theory of moral valuation.

(The) "Way" (in Taoism) – See **fate**.

About the Author

Mark Jablonowski is a professional risk manager, researcher, and writer. During his 30-year career, he has published over 100 articles on the analysis, treatment, and economics of risk. His previous books include *Precautionary Risk Management: Dealing With Catastrophic Loss Potentials in Business, the Community and Society* (2006) and *Risk Dilemmas: Forced Choices and Survival* (2007), both published by Palgrave Macmillan. Mr. Jablonowski is Director of **naturalrisk.org**.

Index